L.L. Bean
Family
Camping
Handbook

L.L. Bean
Family
Camping
Handbook

KEITH McCAFFERTY

The Lyons Press

For photography credits, see page 171

First Edition

Printed in Canada

Designed by Compset, Inc.

10   9   8   7   6   5   4   3   2   1

Library of Congress Cataloging-in-Publication Data
McCafferty, Keith.
     L.L. Bean family camping handbook / Keith McCafferty.
        p.   cm.
     Includes bibliograchical references and index.
     ISBN 1-55821-880-7
     1. Camping Handbooks, manuals, etc.   I. L.L. Bean, Inc.
II. Title.   III. Title: Family camping handbook.   IV. Title: L.L. Bean
family camping handbook
     798.54—DC21   00-26718
                                                                              CIP

Contents

This book is for my father, who put up the tent in the rain, and it is for my mother, who burnt her stockings by the campfire, waiting for her sons to come back from the river.

It also is for my wife, Gail, my daughter, Jessie, and my son, Tom, for bearing with a man who is his father's son, and for not complaining too loudly that it was asking too much of 40-year-old canvas to keep their sleeping bags dry.

Preface

Camping is a haven of tranquility for families that are fragmented by work, school, and the pace of daily living. That has never been more true than it is today, as we struggle to maintain equilibrium in the rush of the twenty-first century. The campground remains one of the last places where different generations can come together without distractions, to work with each other in a spirit of pioneer cooperation, gathering wood, fetching water, deciding which fork of the trail to take, and by so doing, cement a bond that is the richest reward of the experience.

The *L.L. Bean Guide to Family Camping* is designed to start you down the path toward realizing this reward with your own family. It serves as an introduction both for curious prospective campers, whose previous experience may be limited to throwing a sleeping bag onto the grass in the backyard, as well as for parents who already know the joys of camping but remain skeptical about striking off into the outdoors with children.

The text of the book is separated into four sections for easy reference. The Introduction and first chapter offer, respectively, an encouraging prod to get you out the door and a guide for what you can expect at the end of the road. Camping has changed over the last few decades and is not always the simple matter of pitching a tent beside the nearest river or lake that it was for our parents. Questions about costs, camping methods, and gear are answered in Chapters 2 and 3, together with tips for packing up and traveling with children. Use this first section as a navigational aid to help you plan and sort through the myriad choices among campgrounds and camping equipment to find the combination that will provide your family with a satisfying experience.

The second section of this book leads you step by step through a family outing, with chapters on choosing campsites and pitching camp, cooking, relaxing around an evening campfire, and turning in for the night—for the uninitiated, not quite the simple matter of crawling into the bed at a vacation hotel. Such ethical considerations as quiet hours and no-trace camping skills are covered, and laced throughout are suggestions for getting children involved.

Because camping should be a learning process, in the third section of the guide the accent is on nature, with an emphasis on hiking, fishing, and wildlife viewing. The chapters that follow offer a counterpoint; nature's sooth-

Family hiking and camping bring generations together and help to build self-confident children.

Step-by-step planning can help make your family camping adventure a satisfying and memorable experience.

ing balm for the rigors of urban life sometimes demands its own application of ointments when the mosquito strikes, the rain falls, a fishhook gets embedded not in the trout but in your son's hand, or the leaf of poison ivy your daughter touched leaves an itchy souvenir. The section concludes with a few cautionary words for parents who may be misled into thinking that by purchasing the newest tent or following the blueprint of a guidebook, they can walk a perfectly smooth path while living in the outdoors. The fact is that plans go awry and no camping trip is quite like any other; you cannot adjust climate controls to draw a cool curtain across the sun or reduce the heat of a cooking fire the same way you can turn down an oven at home. I think that accepting the spontaneous aspect of camping takes somewhat more adjustment on the part of the adult, who is used to control, than the child. Kids adapt to camping the way ducklings slip instinctively into water (including getting their feet wet, no matter how often you warn them not to!), and sometimes it may simply be wiser to follow wherever the river or the day takes you.

The reference section at the back of the book is filled with information that will be of practical use to campers at any level of experience. Because we all tend to forget things in the last-second crush of packing, it includes checklists for camp gear, cookbox, and medical kits. Provided as well are lists of selected outdoor learning schools, conservation organizations,

Camping brings you closer to the rhythms of the natural world and can foster mental and spiritual renewal.

Sharing the tradition of camping with our children strengthens their appreciation of the natural world and helps them to understand their place in it.

magazines, and books that stress family camping themes. The section concludes with an index of state and federal agencies that list camping opportunities and accept reservations.

I hope the *L.L. Bean Guide to Family Camping* encourages you to cancel motel reservations and buy a tent instead. Camping is a simple way of living that not only strengthens family ties but serves as an introduction to a world as yet untarnished by the hand of man. I know that I have always been happiest in those places where warmth is made with an ax and the striking of a match. Forty-some years of struggling with recalcitrant tents and sleeping on hard ground have not been able to dim my appetite for the clean breath of a mountain wind or the dank scent of a forest, or dampen my appreciation for the inheritance of wild country that makes this journey of spiritual renewal in nature possible.

The fate of such places will soon rest in the hands of our children. If this book results in even one parent passing down the camping traditions that serve to deepen our appreciation of the natural world and strengthen the commitment to preserve it for future generations, then my words will not have been wasted.

SECTION

I

Getting Started

INTRODUCTION

The Rewards of Family Camping

*"God sends children for another purpose than merely
to keep up the race—to enlarge our hearts . . .
and to bring round our firesides bright faces,
happy smiles and loving, tender hearts."*

MARY BOTHAM HOWITT

My baptism as a camper took place on the south bank of Michigan's Au Sable River in 1955, not long after my second birthday. I use the word "baptism" in a literal sense; the tent my father and I slept in was of World War II vintage and may well have withstood storms in Normandy, but after a decade of peace it had let its guard down considerably. Feeling raindrops fall onto my face through holes in the canvas remains one of my earliest memories, a sensation that would be repeated in other leaky tents and in other campgrounds that extended from the Bay of Fundy, off the coast of Maine, to Montana's Big Hole River, from Buckhorn Lake in Ontario to the Great Smoky Mountains.

Each June, Dad loaded our old jalopy with gear until the rusted springs groaned. In those early years we were usually bound for Michigan, and my little brother and I would fall asleep in the backseat and wake up the next morning to our mother's voice, keeping Dad awake after he had driven all night long. Then we'd roll down the windows to drink in the scent of the pines, and because our home was in the shadow of steel mills where the skies were gray and the air smelled of ash, it was like dreaming and opening your eyes in a new land.

I had a secret place over the hill from the tent, where a spring flowed across cedar roots before merging with the river. Over the years I would catch my first trout there, I would write my first bad poem there, I would kiss my first girl. You could sit on the bank, hidden under the canopy of the cedars, and dream of all the great places you wanted to go in your life and all the fine things you wanted to do. Of course, I didn't know then that I was already where I wanted to be, that someday I would look back upon that place and those times, that long month of summer when the tent was pitched and the white noise of the city stopped, as the best of my life.

In camp there was no traffic, no television, no radio, no telephone. Instead, you listened to the mercurial rhythms of the river, the silence of the pines, the snap of fire. In the evening we sang songs, reflecting in the embers a vision of American family life little changed from that of our pioneer ancestors.

My father grew up during the Depression, fought in the war, and worked as a railroad engineer. He would do anything in the world for us.

Early camping experiences create memories that last a lifetime. The first fish, caught on a dry fly, will be remembered as one of life's best moments.

But his job kept him away from home quite a bit. At times he could be distant, gruff, and uncommunicative. He was self-reliant to a fault. The car had to be packed just so before our camping trips and there was no helping him. But once the tent was up, he relaxed. He taught us to cast a fly rod, to split wood with an ax, to identify snakes by the patterns on their scales. Following him downriver in oversize waders, my brother and I held his hands where the current pressed deepest. When we hiked back to camp after dark the lantern would be burning, hanging from a tree stub, and my mother would step out of the tent to admire the gleaming flanks of the trout. We were a closer family then than at any other time of year.

It is this heritage of camping, and of togetherness, that I have tried to pass along to my own family, to my wife, Gail, daughter, Jessie, and son, Tom.

Camping is not just another form of outdoor recreation. It is a way of living. Alone, it nurtures a sense of autonomy and self-reliance, as one must learn to make a home out of a scrap of canvas and deal with broken lantern globes, biting insects, and the vagaries of weather. Traveling with family, camping engenders a spirit both of cooperation and dependence on each other.

When my wife and children and I pitch camp, it's Tom's job to put up the dome tent while Jessie, who is younger, arranges padding and sleeping bags. If we've brought our big cabin tent, all four of us are needed to steady the poles. We must work in concert to get it erected. We know our places and after a few trips, no words of direction are necessary. Packing up also is accomplished with unspoken teamwork, at least after the obligatory prompting (or three!) to get the kids moving.

Then, too, people draw together in times of adversity. I don't want to give the wrong impression of camping—it's a lot of fun. But if you have car trouble or are forced to stand shoulder to shoulder underneath a tiny tarp while the rain pours down, you commiserate together. You also work toward solutions together.

Camping re-opens avenues of communication that close all too easily under the pressures of work and the bustle of modern life. In camp, a sister can't hide from her brother in her room. A husband and wife who have grown apart can't retreat into their busy schedules. A family that sits together in silence before the TV is forced to talk before the fire. Camping offers a glimpse into life as it used to be, when American families lived in one-room cabins and worked side by side in the fields, when parents educated their own children, and family members boosted each other's spirits by telling stories and singing songs.

A few summers ago, an old friend from Florida became worried that she hadn't been able to spend enough time with her daughter, who was going through a period of adjustment at a new school. Her son was a champion swimmer and drew most of the family's attention. Karen's solution was to take her daughter, Carly, on a two-month camping trip across the country. By the time they reached our home in Montana, Karen said she felt closer to Carly than she had in many years.

Another friend loaded her teenage son and daughter into a compact car to begin a cross-country camping trip from the District of Columbia to California, because she wanted them to see our country at ground level, instead of at 30,000 feet from the seat of an airplane. One morning, her children parted the tent flap near the Custer Battlefield, where poppies bloomed on the endless flow of prairie grasses in the Crow Reservation of central Montana; the next morning they awoke to a summer snowstorm at 11,000 feet on the Beartooth Highway. A few hours later they were pitching their tent under a blazing sun near the Lamar River in Yellowstone National Park, while bison placidly grazed below the forested slopes of the Absaroka Mountains.

What a marvelous gift to her children, to show them that even as urban parts of our nation become homogenized with strip malls and chain restaurants, with one motel room pretty much reminiscent of the last, that land retains both its identity and history. Is there a better way of teaching your children about our shifting tableau of geography, our changing index of trees, birds, and animals? Or a less expensive one? I doubt it.

But we are hurrying down the road too quickly. Your first camping expedition need not last a month or cover a country. It can be as simple as an overnight trip to the nearest lake or stream. And it's never too late or too early to start. Gail and I took our daughter on her first camping trip when she was two months old. At two years plus, our son was already the veteran of half a dozen outings, several of them fall trips when the thermometer dipped into the teens at night. Camping with children is nothing to fear, as I hope the pages of this guide will reveal to you.

Camping with grandparents is rewarding in a different way. Instead of your children seeing their forebears only in the context of holidays, place settings for ten, and adults sitting on sofas, speaking of family history that holds no meaning for them—*instead of looking at grandparents as old people who hold out the promise of gifts*—they get to know them as respected mentors, still revered for their knowledge.

Camping can take us to some of the most beautiful places on earth, like the alpine lakes of the Wind River Range in Wyoming.

My father's arthritic fingers were clasped over my son's hand when he caught his first trout from our camp on Montana's Gallatin River, in the same stretch of water where he had taken me fishing nearly 30 years before. A couple of summers later, it was Jessie's turn to hold his hand while she waved an outsized fly rod. His touch will resonate throughout their lives and prove more valuable and enduring than any Christmas gift he could have given them.

Confidence, communication, cooperation. Building bridges of trust through dependence and common work. Discovering our country and its history. Learning outdoor living skills. Cultivating an appreciation of nature. Having fun. These are a few of the family themes of camping touched upon in this book. But there are practical considerations to attend to as well. One can't go camping until one has found a place to camp. The first chapter will examine the evolution of our pastime and help steer you through the labyrinth of possibilities to choose the right place to spread your sleeping bags.

CHAPTER
1

The Changing Face of American Camping

> *"I am glad I shall never be young without wild country to be young in. Of what avail are forty freedoms without a blank spot on the map?"*
>
> ALDO LEOPOLD

The tent pitched on the shore of a secluded lake, a fire on the gravel bar, the teeth of the Rockies spearing a starry heavens—that is a portrait of American camping sold by pickup-truck makers on magazine back covers. It is not one advertised by the National Park Service. Summer camping at the turn of the century can indeed be a remote site at the water's edge. But it also can be wall-to-wall company, chained-down picnic tables, generator hum, numbered asphalt parking tongues, and tents pitched on cordoned off, rectilinear gravel pads. Finding a space in some popular campgrounds may involve Internet searches and long-distance telephone calls, even making reservations up to a year in advance.

This has not happened everywhere; fortunately, overcrowding remains the exception rather than the rule. However, it would be a disservice to begin this book by suggesting that camping has not changed over the past 50 years. Camping *has* changed—not so much the experience itself, but the logistics involved in finding a good campsite. According to the U.S. Census Bureau, camping has become the fourth most popular participatory sport in the nation, with 64 million people pitching tents and hauling trailers each year. The popularity of camping has made it imperative that today's parents do a little more homework than mine did before turning the key in the ignition. Great camping is out there, but searching for a

Though it's not as easy as it once was, today's families can still find secluded campsites like this one.

secluded campsite is like looking beyond the chain restaurants and strip malls to discover the real America. You just have to turn over a few more stones to find it.

PLANNING YOUR TRIP

In the reference section at the back of this book, you will find a list of state and federal agencies to write or call for camping booklets and information. I've also included phone numbers for reservations and a selected library of reference works. Don't overlook the Internet, either.

If you are new to camping, you might be surprised to discover just how much information is available to help in your choices. For example, if you live in Dakota country and think it would be nice to spend a week camping in the Pacific Northwest to refuel with salt breezes, the best place to start your trip is the local bookstore or library. If helpful camping guides are unavailable, ask a reference librarian to request a book on library loan called *The Complete Guide to Pacific Northwest Camping* by Tom Stienstra, which gives descriptions of more than 1,400 campgrounds.

Meanwhile, make phone calls to request camping packets from the state and federal agencies listed in the reference section, as well as area chambers of commerce. Log on to the Internet for a key-word search. Soon you'll have accumulated a drawerful of information, including maps that detail the layouts of individual campgrounds along the coast. You will discover

Not every moment in camp needs to be structured. Free time often can be the best time of all.

that by calling a single phone number, (800) 452-5687, you can reserve sites up to 11 months in advance in any of 61 state parks located in Washington and Oregon. If you know someone who has camped in a park they enjoyed and can remember the number of a preferred loop or site, you can request it, along with a second choice, on your application form.

Children can and should get involved in this planning process. Show them on the map where you are headed. Encourage them to learn more about the area where you intend to camp with trips to the local bookstore and library. Have them check out a book about an animal they particularly want to see or the Indian tribe that originally inhabited that country. Buy a field guide to reptiles or mammals or birds, so that you and your family can expand your knowledge of the local fauna. Older kids can help with Internet research. If our family is any indication, kids are probably better at coaxing information from the computer than their parents.

Ask what your children want to do and have them write down a list of priorities. You may be surprised that many kids prefer campground activities such as building sand castles, swimming in the lake, playing Whiffle ball or Frisbee in a nearby field, or even playing card games on the picnic table to taking daily sightseeing tours and hikes. Kids like meeting and playing with other kids in camp, too. Many parents make the mistake of trying to schedule camping vacations strictly, with too much time on the road or on the trail and too little time for relaxing. To keep your kids happy, it might be wise to schedule a few more days for in-camp fun than you had originally intended.

Before the trip, spend an hour or so in the backyard familiarizing the children with camping equipment. Have them help put up the tent and teach them to roll up their sleeping bags. Discuss sleeping arrangements in the tent and have each child write his or her name on a sleeping bag and pad. Kids appreciate having their own gear to take care of and their own private space in the tent, just as they like their personal property and own bed at home.

Have each child fill a small box with books, games, playing cards, drawing paper, crayons, pencils, journals, favorite book and music tapes, and any other small toys they choose. When it's time to pack the car, children can transfer the items in their boxes to their school backpacks and keep them handy during the trip. It's also a good idea to have them write down the addresses of friends and relatives, so that they can send postcards home from the trip.

Camping Opportunities

Thousands of campgrounds stretch across the nation. Some are at the end of dirt ruts and offer nothing more in the way of conveniences than a pump handle and a privy with a door that won't close. Others have live-in hosts, showers, laundry facilities, electrical hookups, and a complete schedule of organized activities.

Public campgrounds are managed by federal, state, and local agencies. The National Park Service, Bureau of Land Management, National Forest Service, National Wildlife Refuge system, and individual state park systems all offer many camping opportunities. Counties and townships also manage campgrounds. Most public campgrounds are geared toward tent camping, although many offer a limited number of hookups for recreational vehicles.

National Park campgrounds are invariably clean and efficiently run. Most provide amenities such as bathrooms with electrical lighting. Sites are well patrolled and campers must observe strict quiet hours (usually between 10 P.M. and 6 A.M.), which means you won't have to worry about noisy neighbors or disturbing generator hum. As a bonus, park rangers lead nature walks and host evening campfire programs that are geared to both children and adults.

On the down side, because of concerns about erosion and preserving vistas for sightseers, camps are often tucked back into the forests, away from the rivers, lakes, and breathtaking vistas that these parks are noted for. Campsites are often pre-assigned at the gate and tend to be small, eroded by foot traffic, and built close together, although there are many exceptions. National Park campsites usually come at a relatively high sticker price, too.

Popularity is another consideration. During peak summer months, most national park campgrounds fill up daily. The smaller campgrounds are usually first come, first served; some larger campgrounds offer reserved sites (for information on reserving campsites, see the reference section).

National Forest Service and Bureau of Land Management campgrounds range from remote and extremely primitive sites to well-maintained facilities with live-in campground hosts. Many Forest Service campgrounds strike a good balance between comfort and rugged outdoor living, offering well-spaced sites in a pristine setting, while providing basic amenities such as purified water, picnic tables, and, sometimes, indoor plumbing. They also tend to be less pricey and less crowded than national and state park campgrounds. Many primitive forest and BLM camps are free.

Quite often, you can find overflow forest campgrounds outside park borders, built for campers who have arrived too late to secure a park campsite. Some are no better than parking lots. But the farther you get from park entrances, the more spacious the campgrounds tend to be. For example, the road that follows the Shoshone River from Cody, Wyoming, to the east entrance of Yellowstone National Park passes through some of the nation's most spectacular scenery, and the Forest Service campsites along the riverbank are strung out like emeralds pinned to a silver necklace. Vacationers pass these half-empty campgrounds at 70 miles an hour, rushing to grab spaces 40 miles down the road that will be half as big, twice as expensive, and much less abundant in scenic charm.

State park campgrounds are often among the most posh. A number I've visited on the Oregon coast have beautifully situated and well-spaced campsites; one park had walk-in sites on a bluff overlooking the surf. On the other hand, the most densely

Campground Buzz Words

As you negotiate the pages of road atlases, campground directories, and books when searching for campgrounds, it helps to understand a few key words commonly used to describe the facilities:

- *Full hookup* indicates that the campground offers electrical hookups for recreational vehicles (RVs). Tent campers should always check the ratio of tent sites to RV sites with hookup. A high ratio of RV sites usually indicates a more urban camping experience, which is not what most tent campers are looking for.
- *Dumping facilities* are underground waste disposal sites for RVs and trailers.
- *Resort* doesn't identify a campground per se. However, many resorts do offer camping, but it usually won't be a wilderness experience.
- *Primitive* campgrounds offer no hookups, no flush toilets, and sometimes no purified water. They may or may not have picnic tables. About all you can count on are pit toilets.
- *Group tenting sites* are large sites for crowds, generally in the open.
- *Walk-in sites* are far enough from the campground parking area that you will need to tote your supplies. In some campgrounds, the walk-in sites are reserved for hikers and bicycle campers.
- *Wooded* indicates that the campground is built in a forest, which usually means a buffer of trees separate the sites, offering more privacy.
- *Open* indicates the campground is built in a field, on the beach, or on a meadow of prairie grasses. The view of the countryside or ocean may compensate for the lack of privacy.
- *Flush tiolets* flush (usually).
- *Pit toilets* range from dilapidated outhouses to cinder block palaces with chalet roofs, but both offer views of a hole in the ground. Never count on finding toilet paper in an outhouse. Bring a couple of rolls from home.

crowded campground I've ever stayed in was an Oregon state park, also on the coast, where tenters slept cheek to jowl, in the manner of Japanese businessmen cocooned in capsule motels in Tokyo. So it pays to do your homework first.

Municipality, township, and county campgrounds are sleepers, unmarked on most maps and unheralded by campground directories. They tend to be small, inexpensive, and surprisingly private. You can find them in the Yellow Pages of the telephone book.

Privately operated campgrounds offer an alternative to those run by public agencies. Many are no more than glorified rest stops off the highways, catering to overnight travelers. Others are strictly RV parks, where your evening fire, if permitted, will not cast its reflection upon tent walls, but rather upon the gleaming surfaces of aluminum siding. The popular KOA chain offers examples of campgrounds with a resort atmosphere, including showers, laundry facilities, putting greens, a general store, and other amenities that urbanize the experience. But it's unwise to generalize. Our family has visited many private campgrounds, including some on the Maine coast and others in Indian reservations out West that offer well-spaced campsites in remote settings.

Woodall's Campground Directory (see reference section) is updated annually and provides detailed information about thousands of private campgrounds across the nation.

What Kind of Experience Are You Looking For?

Choosing a campground should be based on family priorities. Not all of us are looking for the same experience. If you and your children love to fish, you may be willing to bypass sites on a picturesque alpine lake that freezes solid in winter for one on a mosquito-ridden pond that is dimpled with the rings of rising trout. Some first-time campers may feel insecure in a primitive forest campground accessed by poor roads, and would utter a sigh of relief if they could trade solitude for the peace of mind found in a well-regulated facility with a live-in campground host. Others aren't looking for any kind of wilderness experience at all. They desire nothing more than to pull their trailer onto a manicured lawn, set out a barbecue grill, and split time between the jet ski and the golf course.

Sensibilities must also be taken into consideration. Most men I've shared a tent with are perfectly content to stay in your basic water-pump and outhouse campground; some women I've camped with were not as happy with such Spartan facilities. Children who have been brought up in tents seldom complain, regardless of gender. But if you are new to camping and have a teenager who takes one look at the pit toilet and shakes her head in disgust, the odds of a first outing spawning a second will be considerably enhanced if you are willing to sacrifice a bit of nature for the basic plumbing offered in another campground down the road.

As a rule, however, kids are not as critical as adults. It makes little difference to them if you pitch your tent in the campground's most spacious site or the one that is most cramped, the

Sometimes the perfect camp experience is one that requires little or no set-up time, like this beautifully maintained campground on Casco Bay, Maine—the perfect setting for a family reunion.

one with the best vista or a site that is tucked into the forest. They can get just as big a kick out of camping in the backyard or a nearby lake as they will in Yosemite National Park. In fact, a local lake is often the best choice for novice campers. It's easy to pack for, quick to get to, and you can easily return home for a special event or to retrieve something you forgot to take. When I was a child, we often spent the week before Labor Day camping at Leesville Lake, an hour's drive from town. My father would visit us in the evenings and his days off work. This last hurrah of fishing, swimming, and horsing around with other camp children was a great way to end our summer vacation.

This alternative is something to keep in mind when you catch yourself wavering on taking a longer trip because the car engine has been acting up or you have too many obligations at home.

AVOIDING THE CROWDS

The best way to avoid the summer crush of vacationers is to camp in spring or fall, during semester breaks, or on three-day weekends that the children have off from school. During peak summer weeks, avoid the most popular destinations and seek out-of-the-way campgrounds that take a little more driving to reach.

Parents who work Mondays through Fridays are often faced with the daunting task of begining a vacation on a weekend, when campgrounds are most crowded. One solution to this problem is to make campground reservations in advance for the weekend only. That leaves you free to explore other places during the week, when the odds of finding open campsites are much higher.

MAKING FRIENDS

One of the most significant changes in the camping experience has nothing to do with the place you pitch your tent. It is the time you spend living in it. The average length of a family vacation has dropped to four days, down from two weeks only a couple of decades ago. Forging friendships can be difficult when paths cross for such a short time.

For a child, camping offers the perfect chance to explore the natural world with family and friends.

The layout of most modern campgrounds doesn't help this situation. Numbered campsites engender a that-is-your-space, this-is-my-space attitude, and we instinctively respect others' privacy as we skirt our way to the rest room or take the path to the lake. This is a shame, because one of camping's richest rewards is the people we meet.

Making friends is more a state of mind than anything else. Children are the best ice breakers. When I was a boy, our family went on a vacation to Maine, on the strength of my father's desire to catch an Atlantic salmon. He did not end up catching a salmon, but in our hopscotch manner of looking for them we discovered a small, privately operated campground on a bluff overlooking the Bay of Fundy. We were the owners' first customers. They had a daughter, Becky, who was a year younger than I was (I was 9 or 10 then) and in the way children become instant friends, we spent many hours together wandering the fields near her farmhouse. Much to her parents' horror, I showed her the best places to catch snakes. She, in turn, taught me the undertow on a swing set, where you run underneath as you are giving someone a push. There was a moment during that week when, for the first time in my life, I discovered that the way a young girl's hair looked curled against her neck was infinitely more interesting than the stripes on the back of a garter snake.

Although I never visited Sunshine Shores Campground again, my parents returned several times and became friends with the owners, who kept a photograph of us on their mantle for years.

That childhood idyll, and the indelible memory that became our family's inheritance, would not have happened unless our family had treated camping both as an adventure and as a way to meet new people.

Making friends is easier in campgrounds composed of like-minded souls. At Jenny Lake Campground under the eyetooth of Grand Teton, for example, most campers carry backpacks in their cars. One way to meet people is to unfold a backcountry map on the top of your picnic table and ask your neighbor if he is familiar with the trail that goes from, say, String Lake to Hidden Falls. If a sympathetic chord is struck, soon enough you may find the corners of the map pinned down by a couple of cold ones and accommodations made to increase the size of your hiking party the next morning.

One of my most enduring friendships started as a chance acquaintance when I was carrying a fly rod back to camp.

"Well, how did it go?"

The young man who asked the question had a shock of long black hair and a look of bemused resignation on his face. When I said, "Not too good," he shook his head in condolence. The trout were on strike, he told me, but it didn't matter anyway because all of the big ones held him in contempt.

"They like to rise a few inches from my fly just to torment me," he said wearily. Every syllable he uttered seemed to carry the weight of a great world sadness. He said a man just had to laugh, that was the best medicine.

Twenty-three years have passed since that introduction, in which I have heard Mike Cjaza laugh at his own pessimism from Montana's Bighorn River to the Penobscot River in Maine, to the River Don in Scotland. Today, I would rather share a tent and a river with him than almost anyone else in the world.

CONTINUING THE TRADITION

The campground where I met my friend Mike is Madison Junction in Yellowstone National Park. I mention this because Madison Junction symbolizes the changing face of camping in America, embodying many of the trappings that, for me anyway, tend to diminish the experience if you let them. With more than 200 sites, this campground is too big for intimacy. It is set back on a wooded bluff where you can't see the river. The office attendants won't let you pick your own campsite. The fire grates are poorly ventilated and pretty worthless for cooking. To boot, in the quarter century I have been camping there, close to half the trees have come down, having fallen victim either to fire or the ravages of a bark beetle infestation that swept like a wave through these forests many years ago and turned the pine needles to rust.

Having said that, I must admit that some of the best times of my life have been spent there. My parents are in their seventies now and very seldom camp anymore. But it has become something of a tradition to bring all the generations of our family together in this campground for a few days in October. My mother still enjoys the campfire and the smoke reciprocates, following her wherever she positions her chair. My wife loves the way the last light lays a sheen upon the mirror of the river, and after dinner she goads me into tuning the guitar and leads the family in song. And my children, Tom and Jessie, are here and there, as always.

Come the afternoon, Tom will turn the wall of the tent into a backstop for Whiffle ball. A stump will be first base. If you touch the tree behind the pitcher's mound, you're on second. Home plate will be a floor mat from the car. But third base is sometimes a little iffy; Tom will tend to call himself safe, but when Jessie comes to bat and knocks a good one, she will be mysteriously out, even though she stands in the same spot. This doesn't sit very well with her, and the game will end in a huff.

As for my father, he putters about the stove in the morning, and there is a bend of the river over

The torch of family camping can be passed on early in life. This young camper is already a veteran.

the hill where he can still show us a thing or two about catching trout. But who was holding whose hand across the deep part changed a long time ago; I'm the one who leaves the river last now. And I'm the one who sits alone before the embers, after everyone else has retired to the tent.

It occurs to me at these times that there is something fundamentally reverent about camping that the turning of the century cannot change. It is a feeling of connection rather than any conscious thought, a sense of one blood with the aboriginal hunters and wanderers who left tepee rings in the deposits of the glaciers. They, too, came to this river, and listened. They, too, looked to these stars, and wondered.

Built on old ashes, our fires send smoke to the sentinels of their spirits.

CHAPTER 2

Walls in the Wilderness

*". . . [W]hatever special nests we make—leaves and moss
like the marmots and birds, or tents or piled stone—we
all dwell in a house of one room—the world with the
firmament for its roof—and are sailing the celestial
spaces without leaving any track."*

JOHN MUIR

Food, water, fire, shelter. Of these four basic requirements needed to sustain life outdoors, the one of most immediate concern for first-time campers is shelter. The
ever-expanding spectrum of choices include tents, pop-up tent trailers, travel trailers, truck campers, camper vans, and motorhomes, along with more esoteric offerings such
as tepees, lean-tos, and yurts.

Tenting remains the quintessential camping experience for that most fundamental of reasons—
it involves the most camping. Fetching water from the spring, chopping wood, cooking on coals,
pumping up a lantern, sitting around a fire in the evening, huddling under a rain fly, and snug-
gling into a sleeping bag at night—that's what camping is. The amount of time your family spends
in these activities depends, to a very large extent, upon the thickness of the walls you erect to
keep the elements at bay. Put another way, the actual amount of time you spend camping de-
creases in direct proportion to the number of home conveniences you carry inside those walls.

For these reasons, families would be well advised to give tent camping a try. Like all worth-
while ventures, it entails a bit of work. But learning outdoor living skills sustains the thread
that connects us to those who trod these paths in history. It deepens our appreciation for the
mercurial mood swings of the natural world that we can shut our doors against by hauling a
trailer into wilderness. And of all the methods, tenting is the least expensive way to camp.

Tenting remains the quintessential camping experience for the most fundamental of reasons—it involves the most camping.

TENTS

My introduction to tenting was a two-man, Army-issue scrap of moldy canvas. You could count the stars through holes in its roof. It leaked so much during my inaugural night of camping that I woke up beside my father in a pool of rainwater. Some time toward morning he became aware of my shivering and carried me out to the car, where I joined my mother and baby brother, who were curled up in the back seat. Dad went back to the tent and looked for a dry side to lie down on. Finding none, he spent the next day patching the tent with my mother's needle and thread.

This was the first skirmish my father would have with tents in what soon became an all-out war. The next year he ditched the Army tent in favor of a canvas umbrella tent, which had the advantages of being big enough to sleep the whole family, as well as being new and therefore temporarily waterproof. To put up the umbrella tent, you had to first stake out the corners and then crawl inside with a Rube Goldberg contraption of steel poles. You then had to hinge them in a certain way and place the center pole in a special cup of reinforced canvas. In theory, your work was pretty much finished after that. You could utter a few magic words and with a push the tent would pop up like an umbrella.

In practice, it never went so simply as that. My father would crawl inside the tent and we would hear a good deal of muttering—of words that were decidedly not magic—as the struggle began. Imagine a cat trying to fight its way out of a paper bag. The tent would bulge, the

Camping doesn't get any simpler than this set-up—or any easier.

beast within would roar, and if you were a child, you would stand sort of helplessly outside, wishing you were anywhere else. And these were the easy times, for, often as not, we pulled into the campground after dark. Then it would fall to me to crawl inside and hold the flashlight while Dad and the tent went the distance.

Today's tents are much more agreeable. Featherweight, ripstop, fire-retardant nylon has replaced the 10- to 18-ounce cotton canvas duck that made the tents of my childhood. In addition to being a fraction of the weight, modern designs have eliminated the need for cumbersome interior superstructure and it is much easier to pitch and strike the tent.

Dome or Pop Tents

Dome tents, originally known as *pop tents,* revolutionized tent design in the mid-1970s. Floor layout can be octagonal, hexagonal, or even square, but the distinguishing feature is the half-moon–shaped dome. The tent is raised with only two or three long poles that arc across the top and either run through nylon sleeves or attach with plastic clips to the outside material. Made of aluminum or fiberglass, the poles come in several sections and are attached with interior shock cord. Some tents are made of rain-resistant material, but many are constructed with lightweight, breathable nylon and are protected by rain flies. These tents can be erected in minutes (one model works on a parachute principle; throw it into the air and it comes down fully assembled). There's no need to stake them down first, so after assembly the tent can be maneuvered around until you've located the ideal spot to pitch camp.

Dome tents resist rain and wind quite well, although it's easy to get into the habit of not staking them down, for which you may pay a dear price. A gust of wind blew mine into Montana's Gallatin River one afternoon. My friend Keith Shein fetched it as promptly as a well-trained Labrador retriever. He shook himself off and after uttering only three words—"You owe me"—he returned to his chair by the fire.

On the down side, the sloping sides of the dome mean that you will hunch over a lot, even in large tents that have standing room directly under the center of the dome.

Family-style Tents

Family-style tents, for lack of a better word, come in a variety of styles descended from the canvas designs of my youth. There are umbrella styles, cottage designs, cabin tents, modified dome designs, and others that defy simple description. The main difference between these tents and their forebears are the fabrics—nylon walls,

Large, six- to eight-person family tents that open with screened sides are a delight for summer camping.

taffeta floors, and, occasionally, canvas poplin roofs—and the superstructure, which usually consists of aluminum tubing.

Family tents are bulkier, heavier, and take a little more time to pitch than dome tents. Most aren't free-standing, so you must stake down the corners before erecting them. Family tents aren't as stalwart in a strong wind as dome designs, but they are roomier for a given floor space, have more standing room, and usually offer better ventilation. Some come with room dividers, awnings, or additional rooms that can be added with zippers.

If you have a large family or expect to spend a lot of time in your tent, a family-style tent would be a good choice. The dome style is more convenient for shorter trips, or on vacations where you're moving camp every couple of days.

Backpacking Tents

There are many specialty backpacking tents on the market, most of them based on a modified dome or geodesic design with arcing poles. Some are as complicated as lunar landing modules. Designed to stand up under harsh conditions, they are typically made for sleeping, keeping your gear dry, and little else. I always keep one on the car just in case I have to overnight unexpectedly, but unless you are considering bicycle or canoe camping, or, of course, backpacking, they don't provide enough room to be a good choice for families.

Tent-buying Basics

When buying tents, look for large, durable zippers; tub-style flooring; interior doors with no-see-um netting; and big windows, to allow for plenty of air circulation. Tight, double- or triple-line stitching usually means good quality. Beware of large tents that come with flimsy aluminum stakes, which is often a sign of inferior quality. Never buy a tent from a sporting goods store or at a garage sale before you have a chance to inspect it when erected.

First-time campers often make the mistake of buying a tent that is too small, although it may seem big enough when you have the family lie down inside it in the store showroom. But in camp, you all will have sleeping bags, which take up considerable floor space. And a little extra room at the foot and on each side will provide space to store gear, as well as providing more room for comfort.

Best-quality tents can cost two or three times as much as knockoffs sold in discount sporting goods stores. A good tent is worth the money, but only if you have it to spend, and only if you intend to use your tent a lot. I have a top-of-the-line, cabin-style tent for va-

A lightweight, packable, two- to three-person, expedition-style dome tent is great for canoeing or kayaking, where space and weight are at a premium.

cations, as well as several good backpacking tents. But I also have a foreign-made dome tent that cost pennies by comparison, and which has given excellent service on weekend camping trips for several years. In the L.L. Bean catalog, you can choose among many tent designs, from inexpensive, serviceable domes to the latest designs. Don't hesitate to call the 800 number for advice. Bean's camping staff is knowledgeable and can help you make the best choice.

Garage sales also are a good source of used tents, and about the only place that you will find canvas tents for sale any more. (Many tent and awning makers still sell heavy canvas wall tents, as well as tepees, but these are specialty items favored mostly by western outfitters and hunters who use them for semipermanent wilderness camps.) I found an old canvas umbrella tent at a sale a decade or so ago and bought it for nostalgic reasons. For all their refinements, nylon tents just don't have the character of canvas. They don't have that musty odor that lets you know you're camping, and there isn't the sense of accomplishment you feel after crawling inside an umbrella tent and getting it to open up. And then there is the way the rain sounds on canvas that is the difference between Sinatra and the saloon singer in a second-tier Vegas casino.

Tent-Camping Vehicles

As camping becomes a way of life, many people find themselves sizing up new or used car prospects with an eye to their utility in the outdoors. Larger minivans are an excellent choice for family campers, offering plenty of room for passengers and gear, especially when one of the bench seats is removed. Sport utilities (SUVs) and larger station wagons are good alternatives. If the choice is between two vehicles, one with a lift gate in the back and the other with cargo doors that pull open to either side, pick the one with the lift gate. It will give you protection from the rain while you're pawing through gear or whipping up lunch at a roadside rest. A tailgate that folds down flat is handy as well, turning into a table for preparing food or seating a small child for changing clothes or shoes.

Four-wheel drive is seldom needed in a family camping car. But high clearance vehicles, including many vans and SUVs, will allow you access on back roads that would rip the mufflers off ground-hugging sedans.

I'd go on, but I must admit my preference reflects a minority view. And in any case, I no longer have that tent. Last year I made the mistake of storing it at my father's house, and he says he mistook the rusted nest of hinged poles for scrap metal, and put it in the alley for the garbage truck to take. Given his history with similar tents, I'm inclined to believe he knew what he was doing.

MOTORHOMES, TENT TRAILERS, AND OTHER WALLS IN WILDERNESS

It would be unfair to dismiss other forms of camping besides tenting without mentioning their merits. Family camping does not just mean parents and children. Grandparents camp, too, and many who are older or disabled would have to stay home if they had to depend solely on tents for shelter. My father has had two knee operations that make the simple acts of ducking into and out of tent doors and getting into and out of a sleeping bag on the floor close to impossible. The small RV he and my mother bought several years ago enables them to continue camping with us once or twice a summer.

Over the age of thirty-five, humans tend to lose about 1 percent of their bone mass every year. Although this degeneration can be delayed by exercise, the fact is that by the time many Americans reach their seventies, brittle, deteriorated bones have made sleeping on the pads we associate with tent camping painful. Recreational vehicles and tent trailers come equipped with thick foam mattresses that reduce the skeletal pressure and, just as important, the beds are set at a convenient height.

Past a certain age, the ability to shut a door and close a couple of windows against the cold or fire up a generator-powered air conditioner becomes more than a mere convenience; it is the only way many people can safely continue to enjoy the outdoors. Trailers and motorhomes also makes sense for families that will be on the road a lot during extended vacations and may find themselves taking the last campsite available late in the evenings or spending the night in public rest areas.

Another consideration is weather. A little rain during a tent camping trip is romantic; a lot of it and people become quarrelsome and exasperated. I lived in Washington for a year and camped extensively on the Olympic Peninsula; although I carried a tent in my old International Travel-All, I don't remember putting it up on more than a couple of occasions. Usually, I simply fished in the rain, cooked dinner on a Coleman stove set on the hood of the car during a break in the clouds, and then, when the rain started back up, crawled inside to read until bedtime. Family camping under those conditions would have been miserable without some sort of hard-sided shelter.

Having a trailer or camper parked in your drive greatly reduces the amount of packing you need to do before a trip. The living and sleeping quarters are ready to go. About all you need to do is buy groceries and occasionally refill the propane tanks. That's something to consider if your work is all-consuming and vacations are limited to weekend getaways.

Lastly, hard-sided vehicles provide a sense of protection tents can't match. While crime in campgrounds is generally not a problem, no one can completely ignore security. And in a deep pocket of country that dips from western Montana into Wyoming and Idaho, it's not only against human thieves that we lock the doors. Grizzly bears have on rare occasions torn apart tents and killed campers. In a few campgrounds along well-traveled bear corridors, only hard-sided vehicles are admitted.

Because the initial cost can be substantial, keep in mind that most types of trailers and recreational vehicles can be rented. So can tents and basic camping gear. Leasing a larger RV doesn't come cheaply, but it's probably a good idea to camp in one for a week or so to see what it's like before investing a lot of money in buying one.

Let's take a look at the advantages and disadvantages of each of these options.

Motorhomes

Class A motorhomes, which are constructed on specially built chassis, are the largest recreational vehicles. Many retired people live in them year-round, towing small cars to drive when the motorhome is moored in camp. They are like yachts in a harbor slip, offering every convenience of home and then some. But big motorhomes can be expensive and unless you own an oil refinery, your bank book will take a hit each time you turn the key. You can't turn them around or park them just anywhere, and many campgrounds and scenic byways have length restrictions that preclude their use.

Lots of families vacation in Class A motorhomes, but you would have to stretch the definition to call it camping.

Class B motorhomes are built on van chassis. They differ from *Class C motorhomes* only because they lack an overhead bed that sticks out over the driver and passenger seats. The boxy old Winnebago was the prototypical Class C motorhome. Its descendants are more aerodynamic, more fuel-efficient vehicles, with better handling on the road. Both Class B and Class C motorhomes are fully self-contained, with propane heaters and kitchen units; electrical power is provided by generators. Although these motorhomes are much more versatile than Class A motorhomes, you still have to resist their conveniences, at least in fair weather, and step outside the door to breathe the scent of nature.

Class B motorhomes offer comfort, safety, and convenience for families that prefer the comforts of home.

Micro-mini motorhomes are smaller yet. Built on truck chassis, some of the 4-cylinder models provide little more than comfortable sleeping quarters, although many contain stoves, bathrooms, air conditioners, and propane heaters. Most have standing room, but there isn't a lot of space to lounge around. That, however, is not altogether a drawback, because it encourages vacationers to spend more time outdoors.

Camper Vans

A conversion van is a regular van to which the builder adds a taller roof and whatever interior improvement he wishes. Conversions built on one-ton cargo vans are as large as small motorhomes and can be as elaborate as the owner cares to make them. They are a good alternative for the craftsman who aspires to having a motorhome but can't afford the price.

Recreational vehicles allow people who aren't interested in "roughing it" to enjoy camping with family and friends. They are especially useful for helping elderly and disabled individuals to enjoy summer outings.

Volkswagen van campers are the "Swiss Army knife" of RV camping—small, but efficient.

Van conversions range in size, the smallest being the familiar Volkswagen camper, which is fully equipped at the factory. These compact vans are the Swiss Army knives of the RV universe. We had a bare-bones model back in the '60s that even my father remembers fondly, despite the fact that he had to replace the entire engine when it seized up during a trip to the Rockies, costing us nearly a week's vacation. Today's VW campers, besides being mechanically more reliable, offer an incredible range of conveniences, from sinks to stoves to overhead, pop-up extensions with full-size beds. They are really too small for a family of four to comfortably live out of, but are a great vehicle to take tent camping. VW vans make lunch or dinner on the road a cinch, offer a cozy retreat for playing cards or reading during bad weather, and have enough lie-down room to nap in at roadside rests.

Travel Trailers

Travel trailers offer the obvious advantage of being detachable, leaving you with a car or truck to drive after making camp instead of a lumbering, ground-hugging motorhome. But that is their Achilles heel as well, because you have to go through the trouble of hitching them up and leveling them out each time you move. Also, the overall length of the rig can get to be a little tiresome to maneuver around. My father sold the old family Airstream for just these reasons.

RV sales have cut into the travel-trailer market, but they remain popular among families that haul them once or twice a summer to semipermanent camps. They also are a favorite of hunters, who park them at trailheads and leave them between days off. Some people have abused camping privileges by leaving their trailers in the best sites for weeks on end and visiting only on weekends; fortunately, many campgrounds have enacted policies prohibiting this practice.

In recent years, fifth-wheel trailers have gained greatly in popularity. They have a forward-overhanging section that hitches directly over the real axle in a truck bed. This makes them tow easily and track better on sharp turns; it also reduces the overall length of the outfit. The disadvantage is the same as it is for any large trailer. It takes a lot of horses to haul them, and a lot of fuel to feed the horses.

Truck Campers

Truck-toppers are removable units designed to sit in the beds of pickup trucks. Larger ones have an overhanging bed that projects out over the cab of the truck. Though they are less costly than similar-sized motorhomes, most are equipped with the same amenities, including propane heaters, stoves, and sinks. They are extremely popular in western states, where rough roads sometimes necessitate four-wheel drive or high clearance.

There are a few drawbacks. Floor space is limited by the width of the truck bed, so there isn't much walking-around room. Taller camper units make the whole rig tipsy. Placing four feet of wind resistance on top of the cab pretty much shoots the gas mileage, too And, of course, passenger space is limited by the seating in the cab.

Despite these disadvantages, truck campers are a practical choice for some campers. If you consider this alternative, avoid the mistake of buying too big a camper, which puts a strain on the engine, brakes, and suspension, and makes the entire rig unwieldy. One solution is to buy a top with an accordion-type extension that raises to full height in camp but folds down for easier driving. Such roof extensions also are options on some vans and motorhomes.

Pop-up Tent Trailers

Tent trailers offer many of the advantages of recreational vehicles, while preserving more of the outdoor camping experience tenters enjoy.

Tent trailers have collapsible sides and either plastic or aluminum tops that lock onto the body for towing and crank to full height in camp. The beds are housed in side wings that slide out from the main body. Some are as luxuriously appointed as larger motorhomes, with such conveniences as showers, refrigerators, kitchen units, toilets, awnings, zip-on rooms that you can add in camp, bicycle and boat racks, outside cargo lockers, sofa-bed layouts, even porta-

Pop-up tent campers offer many of the advantages of recreational vehicles, while preserving more of the outdoor camping experience that tenters enjoy.

ble whirlpool baths. Pop-up trailers operate either off 12-volt car batteries or hook to standard 110-volt electrical outlets. Most come with propane tanks to operate the hot-water heater and stove units, and sometimes even the lights.

At the other end of the spectrum are smaller models that have little besides a take-down table and the extensible wings that make up into camp beds.

Having little wind resistance, tent trailers pull like a whisper, and once you get used to the routine, you can set them up in ten or fifteen minutes. They can be retracted just as quickly.

The elevated sleeping area and ease of hauling make tent trailers good choices for older campers. Kids like them, too; they instantly convert the big beds into playgrounds once the trailer is opened. Screen windows keep tent trailers airy and cool in hot weather, and they can be easily heated either by the furnace system or a lantern.

About the only disadvantages of tent trailers are their prices. A fancy one will cost almost as much as the car you'll need to haul it. There is a good used market, but if the canvas is in good condition, even vintage tent trailers retain their value.

LEAN-TOS

As a camping experience, living in a lean-to constructed of log walls and a cloth front falls somewhere between tenting and renting a small cabin. Inside the walls, you have the comfort of individual beds, a table and chairs, and perhaps even a woodstove to test your pioneer cooking skills. Yet you are never more than a millimeter of canvas away from the elements. In fair weather, you can roll up the cloth so that the entire front stays open.

Lean-tos hold a rustic attraction for parents and children alike. Baxter State Park in Maine has a long-standing tradition of offering rental lean-tos in several campgrounds. My family camped in our first lean-to on Nesowardnahunk Lake near Baxter more than 30 years ago. Although lean-tos are not widely available, they offer a unique experience that every camper should try.

CABINS

Rustic cabins are an option most campers overlook. You won't find them listed in all the brochures and guidebooks, but many national forests quietly offer them for a nominal fee. A few national parks also rent cabins, some with canvas walls. Our family reserves a forest cabin for a long weekend each winter. It is primitive: no water, no electricity, no indoor plumbing. Cooking is done on an ancient woodstove. We have to pack in all our provisions and cross-country ski a little over a mile to reach it.

Is it camping? Perhaps not, but it is a form of pioneer living that offers much the same rewards by bringing families together in a spirit of common work. Cabins are an excellent choice for larger parties and for winter outings, when snow camping with small children can be more hassle than it's worth.

To find out about reserving cabins, contact local forest district headquarters. Weekends tend to book up quickly, so plan your trip well in advance. Be prepared to either hike, snowshoe, or cross-country ski to some cabins. Kids' plastic sleds make the job of hauling gear a lot easier than it would be if your back did all the work. No matter what you hear about provisions, always pack along an extra propane or gasoline lantern. Dark log walls and small windows combine to make most cabins I've stayed in pretty gloomy without the extra light.

Renting a wilderness cabin can be a great way to get a reluctant family involved in outdoor activities. For many, it is a relatively inexpensive way to take a family vacation.

CHAPTER
3

Packing Up, Heading Out

*"Our life is frittered away by detail . . .
Simplify, simplify."*

HENRY DAVID THOREAU

Last autumn, a friend and I stopped at a border crossing between the United States and Canada, near the town of Sweetgrass, Montana. Having nothing to declare, we were briskly waved through and pulled a few yards past the checkpoint to stop and make our lunch before continuing on our fishing trip. The family behind us, a younger couple with three daughters, were not as fortunate. A uniformed guard had them park their stuffed Suburban and unload.

"It looks like you're going to Banff, all right," the guard said straight-faced, after a canoe had been lifted off the roof rack so the cargo doors could be opened. We watched while tents, sleeping bags, backpacks, and an assortment of other gear came tumbling out. By the time Fred and I had finished our sandwiches, the parents were standing beside a mountain of duffel. The oldest daughter was sitting on a cooler with her chin on her fist, having in the span of 20 minutes run through a gamut of emotions, from fear to excitement to utter boredom, and the two little girls were playing jacks on the asphalt. The Suburban chassis was sitting unburdened on its springs, the way a cargo ship floats high in the water after the cranes have finished unloading it. Picking through the gear was the guard in starched uniform, who reminded me of a magpie pecking at a roadkill deer.

Whatever that man was looking for, I'm sure he didn't find it. Having packed my own vehicles to bursting at the outset of a many a camping trip, I knew from experience that the odds of an outsider finding any particular item are exceedingly poor, when you consider that the owner of the vehicle would himself probably have great difficulty locating his coffee pot in the morning.

Why packing has to be so complicated—for a way of life that is seemingly simple—continues to elude me. However, here are a few suggestions that may help keep you from becoming overwhelmed.

When packing for your camping trip, make sure you have included your tent rain fly, tent poles, and stakes, along with your tent.

CHECKLISTS

Preparing for a camping trip begins with pencil and paper. I separate my list of gear into three columns: essentials, essential non-essentials, and "maybes" (expanded lists of camp gear, cooking gear, food, clothing, and medical kit are provided in the reference section at the back of the book).

Essentials

Essentials for a typical one-week camping trip include:

- Tent, poles, stakes, and ground cloth
- Rain fly
- Sleeping bags
- Sleeping pads
- Pillows
- Cookstove
- Cookbox with pots, pans, utensils, and scrub pad
- Cooler and food boxes
- Lantern and spare mantles
- Extra fuel bottle or propane canister, depending upon type of lantern and stove
- Rain parkas (one per person)

- Backpacks or belt packs for day hikes
- Ax
- Swede or bow saw for cutting logs
- Flashlights (one per person)
- Camp chairs
- Folding knife
- Sportsman's multipurpose tool or Swiss Army knife
- Polarized sunglasses
- Medicine kit
- Sunscreen
- Insect repellent
- Plastic trashcan liners (a hundred and one uses, i.e., emergency parka, emergency waders, water bag, fish bag)
- Duct tape (likewise)
- Water containers
- Fire grill
- Charcoal, matches, and lighter fluid (for cooking and lighting fires from damp wood)
- Lightweight, folding Army shovel
- 100 feet of parachute cord or strong nylon rope
- Bungee cords
- Work gloves

Most basic camping gear can be purchased locally from sporting goods stores, discount chains, and Army-Navy surplus outlets. L.L. Bean offers a full catalog of quality camping gear for all budgets. I've picked up odds and ends at garage sales, too.

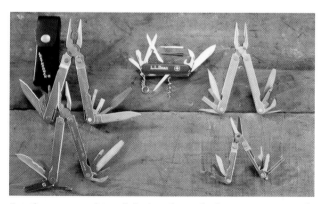

Leatherman tools and Swiss Army knives are great utility tools around camp.

Let's face it. Many of us do not go camping solely for the sake of nature; we camp because it's cheap and our families can vacation for two weeks in a tent for the cost of a single night in a two-star hotel. If you're on a budget, instead of ordering one $40 camp chair, why not buy four folding lawn chairs for the same price? They weigh next to nothing, pack compactly, and are really quite comfortable. And if the lawn chairs are stolen, which happened to us once in a Forest Service campground, you're only out of pocket a few bucks.

My advice, for first-time campers, is to hold off before sinking all of your vacation money into camping gear. Buy the lawn chairs, use the grill from your backyard barbecue, take pillows from home instead of buying camp pillows, and staff your cookbox with skillets and pans that are kitchen castoffs. A couple of years down the road, if it looks like you'll continue camping and have the money, you can invest in better gear.

In warm weather, you can get by with inexpensive sleeping bags (for a discussion of sleeping bags and pads, see Chapter 7). On chilly nights, simply throw a comforter over the top. But don't skimp on sleeping pads, which will reward you with a good night's sleep. And buy a quality tent. The initial outlay will pay off in durability down the road.

Beware of garage-sale lanterns that sport $10 stickers. I've learned from hard experience that most will have defective generators that can't be replaced or have some other terminal disease that renders them no more useful than window dressing. Buy a modern-design lantern, such as the Coleman or the models offered by L.L. Bean. The newer lanterns that use dual-fuel (unleaded gasoline or kerosene) or propane are much more reliable and easy to operate than older designs. Choose the dual-fuel if money matters to you; gasoline is less expensive than propane and, besides, the hiss of a gasoline lantern is one of camping's most venerable songs. A double-mantle, dual-fuel lantern does most of the work in our camp, but on longer trips I often pack a propane lantern for a backup. It's quicker to light, which comes in handy when we pull into camp after dark and need immediate illumination for pitching the tent.

When it comes to stoves, the two-burner Coleman, which has remained virtually unchanged for half a century, is still among the best (L.L. Bean and other companies offer similar designs). What you sacrifice in trunk space is more than made up for by sturdy construction and a fold-open design that permits cooking out of the wind. Having two burners to work on is not a luxury, it's a necessity if the camp cook is serving a family of four or more. I recommend buying one of the wider models (26 inches or so); the burners of compact models are too close together to allow cooking with standard-size pots and skillets.

Gas or propane? Both have advantages. Propane stoves are quicker to light, simpler to operate, and less likely to clog with fuel residue and sputter out on you (the same is true of propane lanterns). Look for propane stoves and lanterns that offer electronic, push-button ignition for easy lighting. The ones from L.L. Bean have adjustable control valves that really work, which is not the case with all propane camp gear I have used.

Gas cookstoves are more economical than propane stoves and, as a rule, are easier to adjust for simmering. Besides giving you better control of the flame, gas stoves capture the spirit of

There is a great selection of coolers available on the market today. Shop around until you find one that fits your needs and budget.

pioneer cooking. Pumping up the pressure, fiddling with the valve, all the tinkering—it just seems more like camping.

Many people use connecting hoses to operate cookstoves and lanterns off an auxiliary propane tank. That arrangement is okay if you have a big rig to haul gear or are planning to stay in the same camp a while. But in bear country, where you have to stow cooking gear in the car when not in use, it's an inconvenience. Fold-up camp kitchens and cookstove tables also are fine if you don't have to worry about anything larger than a raccoon prowling around your camp, but they're too cumbersome when you're on the move or have to consider visitors that make bigger bumps in the night.

Coolers have come a long way from the thin-sided, metal boxes that turned ice into water in a couple of hours. Today, you can buy thick-walled, plastic-sided coolers that actually keep food cold.

Styrofoam coolers, especially those that steak and lobster packers use for shipping, are cheaper and also insulate very well. If you are looking for durability, however, go with the more expensive hard-shell coolers since the Styrofoam ones tend to crack. The noise that Styrofoam coolers make when rubbing against other gear in the car can drive you nuts. Wrap your coolers with towels or blankets—the extra insulation not only keeps them quiet, it helps keep the food colder.

Some coolers have refreezable ice packs that attach onto the lid and sides. That eliminates the need to pack extra ice during weekend trips, but not on longer outings. You can also buy coolers that plug into the cigarette lighter. They may be just the ticket for road trips, but unless you camp in a site with a power outlet, the design is so much wasted technology.

Clothing

Most campers wind up packing too much clothing. I have returned from many camping trips wearing the same shirt and pants I started out in, having paused only a couple of times during the week to wash up and change underwear and T-shirts. My wife has finer sensibilities, but they are not so fine as to prevent her from packing all her personal gear into a medium-sized duffel bag. The children take after me. In fact, any child who voluntarily changes clothes more than once during a camping trip of any duration is one I've yet to meet.

To keep the car from becoming overcrowded, have a family rule that each member be able to store all his or her clothing and personal items in a single bag. For a week-long trip, the contents will include a couple of changes of camp clothing, and perhaps one nicer outfit if there's a chance of going out to dinner. Hikers should pack underwear that wicks sweat away from the body and passes it to outer clothing layers, where it can evaporate (see Chapter 8 for a full discussion of outdoor clothing). Underwear fabrics such as polyester and propylene, combined with outer layers made of pile or fleece, keep your skin warm and dry during heavy exercise. They also are good choices for rainy-weather camping because, unlike cotton, they maintain insulating value when wet and dry quickly. Don't forget hats. A cap with a shade brim will suffice for most daytime conditions, but each child will need a fleece or wool cap that pulls over the ears to stay warm at night.

Most hikers wear two socks: a thin, inner liner made of polypropylene or other wicking synthetic, and an outer sock that is a wool blend. This helps prevent the chafing that leads to blisters. Sports-blend socks (Approach, Trail, or Trekking socks available from L.L. Bean) have extra cushioning at the toe and heel and are the best choice if you want to wear only one sock.

There's no reason to pack a lot of clothing even for longer vacations, because you will always be able to find a laundry close by. We've learned, however, that it's smart to pack plenty of socks and underwear. They take up only a little space and give you the option of skipping the wash if stopping becomes too inconvenient.

Shoes

Always pack extra shoes! I use an exclamation point because kids invariably get their shoes wet—my children often have within the first few minutes of pitching camp. Most tennis shoes dry slowly. Prop them up on sticks over a fire and all you'll accomplish is melting the soles or, worse, dropping one into the flames. My daughter has been known to show up in a mountain campground in October with nothing more substantial than sandals to wear. It's something kids just don't think about. There's a safety issue at stake here, too. It's dangerous to wade in streams or squish through muck without foot protection. To avoid having a child go barefoot because she's afraid of being scolded for getting her shoes wet, make certain everyone has one old pair of shoes or sandals for wearing in the water.

A pair of lightweight hiking boots will give you better ankle support than running shoes or tennis shoes and will offer better traction over some types of terrain. Hiking boots are recommended for backpacking or long dayhikes, but for most campground activities boots aren't really needed. My brother and I climbed Maine's Mount Katahdin in low-top Keds when we were boys. Today's athletic shoes are far superior to what we wore and are perfectly adequate for hiking, as well as for light backpacking in dry climates. Those marketed as cross trainers work best, but basketball or tennis shoes with a deep tread for traction are also good.

Essential Non-Essentials

If essential gear includes all you need to make camping work, the essential non-essentials are what you need to make it fun. Sure, camping should be an educational experience for children. But the pace of their lives mirrors our own in these hectic times, and after the tent is up, kids and adults alike need to take a little time out for playing games, reading, or relaxing in a hammock. Essential non-essentials include such odds and ends as air-freshener packets, to make trips to the outhouse more pleasant. They also include the little things that brighten the day, like cut flowers from home to place on the picnic table and turn dinner into a celebration.

Here are a few non-essentials our car is never without:

- Favorite toys and stuffed animals for children
- Playing cards and board games
- Hammock
- Camera
- Comforters
- Whiffle bat and ball
- Frisbee
- Kite
- Binoculars and bird identification booklet
- Books
- Sing-along books
- Air-freshener packets and favorite-brand toilet paper
- Tablecloth and vase of flowers

"Maybes"

These items are the extra gear and toys that add the camel's hump to the top of the station wagon and bring the suspension to its knees. But it's also the "maybes" that can make or break a trip.

Because most campgrounds are near some form of water, it often seems like half the space in our car is taken up with fishing rods, waders, air mattresses, and other water-related gear.

The decision to haul a canoe or raft is not one to make lightly; they add wind resistance, cut into fuel mileage, and make it difficult to open rear cargo doors. But they are your ticket to nature's greatest theme park, providing a silent and unobtrusive entry into natural areas near camp, as well as recreation for the kids. Because of the hassle of hauling canoes or rafts in smaller cars or on longer trips, you can consider renting them. Many fishing shops and outdoor gear stores rent canoes and inflatable rafts at reasonable prices.

Here's an abbreviated list of possibles to consider:

- Rubber raft or canoe and paddles
- Children's flotation mattresses
- Mask, snorkel, and flippers
- Life jackets
- Fishing gear
- Waders and wading boots
- Broom
- Mesh bug tent
- Portable shower
- Folding camp table
- Portable toilets for young children
- Guitar or harmonica

A camp table really isn't mandatory if the campground has picnic tables, but if you are unsure, it's a good idea to take one along. L.L. Bean's roll-up camp tables, consisting of wood slats covered in waterproof vinyl, are remarkably sturdy and offer a compact alternative to bulky aluminum folding tables.

For some people, and in some places—the Maine woods in July, for example—a mesh bug tent can make the difference between a memorable trip and a miserable one. Portable, solar-heated showers will be addressed more fully in subsequent chapters.

We usually have a struggle in our family over bringing the guitar. Since it is bulky and fragile, it has to be packed last, and its inclusion often precludes the driver from being able to see over the top of the gear in the rear-view mirror. My wife argues on behalf of the guitar's contribution to the camaraderie around the evening fire, while I, who have to play it with tender, out-of-practice fingers, say, "It's just one more thing." It usually winds up being one more thing that makes the trip.

Non-Essentials

No portable television, no boombox, no Walkman, and no explanation necessary. Okay, some kids may demand an explanation. Tell them that the point of camping is to listen to the world as it was created. That includes the song of birds, the whisper of wind, the cacophony of crickets, and, sometimes, the sound of silence. If your kids must listen to music, set strict guidelines and have them use headphones or play the car radio with the doors and windows closed, so they won't disturb other campers.

ON THE ROAD

Roof Racks

The roof rack is one of the great inventions of the twentieth century. For a camper, it is nearly as indispensable a piece of gear as a backpack is to a hiker. Not only does the extra cargo space help keep the interior of your vehicle uncluttered, but it gives you a platform to lash down firewood that would otherwise dirty the car. Short of a boat trailer, a roof rack is the only feasible way to transport a canoe or large inflatable raft to the campsite.

Beware of the minimal crossbars that come pre-installed on some vehicles; they may be fine for lashing down duffel, but many won't be wide or tall enough to keep a canoe or john-boat from scraping the paint. If you can afford it, buy a stout carrier with several crossbars.

In addition to a couple of long straps for tying down the canoe, carry bungee (shock) cords in various lengths. They greatly simplify securing firewood and camp gear.

Car-top Carriers

Storing gear inside a car-top carrier is another way to keep the interior of your vehicle from becoming overcrowded. There's a tradeoff involved, of course. Some car-toppers are hard to pack and unload, especially for campers who are vertically challenged or have a particularly tall car. Large, boxy carriers hold plenty of gear, but the wind-resistant design cuts into your mileage. And while slim, aerodynamically shaped car-toppers may look nice, they hold very little in the way of bulky gear. Car "backpacks," made of heavy, vinyl-coated polyester, are the latest trend in carriers. The ones L.L. Bean offers expand to hold a lot of gear, but fold down compactly when not in use. These "backpacks" also hug the roof, making them less wind-resistant than taller carriers.

Thieves are a consideration when you use a car-top carrier. Thefts are rare in campgrounds, but not so rare on the road. We once had our car-top carrier swiped from the parking lot of the Old Faithful Inn in Yellowstone Park, of all places!

Because we often pack a canoe, the car-top carrier stays home on most trips. However, for families who camp out of smaller vehicles, it can be a wise investment.

Cargo Trailers

Another option, and a very good one overlooked by most campers is a small, single-axle cargo trailer with a locking lid. A typical design is about 6 feet long by 4 1/2 feet wide by 2 feet deep, with a locking lid. That size will pack all the nuts and bolts of your camp gear; anything it doesn't hold can be lashed down on the lid with straps and bungee cords. When you pull the trailer, you'll bearely know it's there. Between trips, you can just leave your gear locked in the trailer, ready to go.

On the down side, most cargo trailers are a craftsman's project, though a relatively simple one; many can be bought in kit form from mail-order houses. Even a very small trailer will present parking problems, and the wiring for the tail lights tends to short out sooner, rather than later. But that's a very small price to pay for the advantages a cargo trailer affords.

PACKING UP

Packing the Car

The rule of thumb is to stow heavier camping gear first, such as tents, stoves, fishing tackle boxes, and cookboxes. Make certain the lantern case is wedged upright where it can't rattle or tip over. It's a good idea to wrap the glass globe with a strip of foam or bubble wrap, and pack extra mantles, because the car's vibration will eventually shake them into dust.

Ready access to lunch foods is important, especially when it comes to pacifying younger children. Keep the cooler and the box where you store snacks accessible, so you can get to them without digging. Pack a roll of paper towels, a few paper plates, and some eating utensils into the same box with the snacks and protect them from the sun's rays with blankets, jackets, or pillows.

Leave personal bags sitting on the lawn until the car is packed; they go in last. Have the children load their school backpacks with games, playing cards, drawing materials, and books, and keep them handy.

It's an advantage to have a couple of cargo areas, rather than a single large space where most gear will remain well buried until you've reached camp. Vans are one of the vehicles that give you the option of dividing your gear. Remove the middle bench and store coolers and personal gear be-

Pack large, bulky items into the car first. Keep personal bags handy by packing them last. This leaves the food and games more accessible.

hind the front seats for easy access. That leaves the rear cargo space for your stove, lantern, and other camp gear.

Use the car-top carrier or roof rack to store bulky gear, such as thick sleeping pads, camp cots, and chairs. Some people are very sensitive to the smell of gasoline that can emanate from the fuel canister in a camp stove. If you don't have to cook en route, store the stove inside the carrier as well. Wrap tents or other gear that will be exposed to weather in those blue poly tarps sold in hardware stores; in camp the tarps can double as ground cloths or even rain flies. It's a good idea to leave one side of the roof rack open for stacking firewood found alongside the road. Flat nylon straps are preferable to rope for securing heavy gear, but be aware that shifting loads or rain will eventually cause slack. Stretch a few bungee cords between the straps for good measure; like duct tape, bungee cords are one piece of camp gear you can never have enough of.

Canoes and boats place a great deal of strain on roof racks, not only because of the weight, but because of the wind pressure that builds up in the hollow of the boat at road speeds. I once saw a canoe blown entirely off a car, taking the roof rack along with it. If your roof rack is on the flimsy side, take the precaution of running a strap all the way around the boat and inside the back doors of the vehicle, securing both the craft and roof rack to the car.

One last tip—annoying strap hum can usually be quieted by putting a simple twist in the strap, which will alter the wind flow.

Packing the Cooler

On longer trips, it's a good idea to take a couple of coolers: a larger one for camp food and a smaller one to store drinks and lunches for the road. Soft-sided coolers, such as the ones L.L. Bean offers, are convenient for road lunches. To avoid the mess caused by ice melting in the bottom of the cooler and mixing with food, freeze water in plastic or cardboard half-gallon milk cartons. You also can freeze a quart or half-gallon of juice for drinking a few days into the trip.

Placing frozen cartons in the corners of your cooler and draping a couple of refreezable ice packs on top creates an effective cooling system that should last for several days. Cold air sinks, so always place ice packs or freezer bags of frozen food near the top of the cooler. After the ice melts, cut the top off one of the plastic containers and use it as a bailer for your boat or canoe.

Buy block ice to replenish the cooler. It will last a lot longer than cube ice. Wrap the block in a plastic bag (tall kitchen bags are a good size for general camp use) to keep it from leaking. Regardless of how well you pack ice, count on some of it melting into the bottom of the cooler. Always take the precaution of storing perishable food in freezer bags or Tupperware containers to keep it from being condemned to the bilge water at the bottom of the cooler.

TRAVELING WITH CHILDREN

Two hundred miles into the first long trip my wife and I took with our children, I pulled off the interstate to look for a motel. We had started our trip late and it was approaching midnight. As I stopped the car at the first intersection, I glanced over at Gail. She had her head on a pillow against the passenger seat door. Turning my head, I saw that my son and infant daughter were asleep in the back. I noticed something I had not encountered since Tom had been born three years earlier: utter silence. I fumbled in the glove compartment for a No-Doz, put the van into gear, and turned back onto the highway.

Driving at night is one solution to the problem of keeping children happy during long trips, when getting there is *not* half the fun. It is one my wife does not endorse, but which has worked both for me and my parents before me.

For infants and toddlers, the key to traveling during daylight hours is to divert their attention from the fact that they can't move around freely. In other words, you must give them something to do, because they are in a position where it's difficult to amuse themselves. Gail liked to save up a few inexpensive toys to parcel out during longer drives. Doling out special snacks worked on the same principle, but both were quick fixes for what could prove to be a long day. We found music tapes of kids songs to be more enduring mood lifters, as well as books on tape, which are a godsend on cross-country drives. Our local library had a selection of children's titles, such as E.B. White's classic, *Charlotte's Web*. As they grew older, adventure tales like *Tom Sawyer* and *The Hobbit* were more to their liking. The human voice has an even more soothing effect than the recordings, and we would take turns reading from the book bag until both of us lost our voices.

Road games took on a larger role as they grew up. We stuck mostly to old standbys, such as the license plate game, where each child chooses five states and the first to see all five wins. Another favorite was the game where you give each child a list of ten objects, such as white horse, mailbox, bird on a wire, weathervane, and so on, with the winner being the first to fill his or her list. A game the adults could join in on was "Who am I?", where everyone took turns asking questions like, "Are you a character in a cartoon?" or "Are you extinct?" until the choices were narrowed and somebody guessed right. "Who can stay quiet the longest?" was a game that made the adults roll with fiendish, silent laughter, for which I am sure I will pay someday, when my children are far away and I long for the sound of their voices.

A magnetic chess and checkers board was a hit for several years, and a deck of playing cards became an old standby, both on the road and in camp.

Today the tables have turned somewhat. The children, now teenagers, subject us to their music choices and books on tape. Jessie occasionally balks at going camping unless she can bring a friend, and Tom has reached the age at which almost everything we say is wrong. Of course, it's also the age when he can start driving, and take a little of the burden from his old man and mama.

SECTION
II

Making Camp

CHAPTER
4

Pitching Camp

"After you have exhausted what there is in business, politics, conviviality, and so on—have found that none of these finally satisfy, or permanently wear—what remains? Nature remains."

WALT WHITMAN

Pitching camp begins at home. Don't wait until it's evening in the woods to find out that a tent pole is missing or the directions for assembling the rain fly are incomprehensible. That won't be a problem if you buy quality gear from L.L. Bean or another reputable company. However, it is always a good idea to erect tents and other gear in your backyard in full sunlight, taking time to familiarize yourself with their construction and checking to make sure they are sturdy.

This I've learned the hard way more than twice, but one recent incident stands out in my memory. I was visiting a friend in central Maine. Bernie was a man who would cut out his heart for you if you asked him, and I was not surprised that he offered me his tent and his truck when I told him I wanted to take off for a couple of days camping by myself.

Bernie's truck I declined, on the grounds that it had no turn signals, no gas pedal, and no discernible brakes, among other degenerative diseases. But I packed the tent in the rental car, and late that night spread it out on the ground in the beam of the headlights to assemble. It was a backpacking tent of a peculiar design: it seemed to have both a rain fly and an interior bug screen sewn to the tent's main body. I struggled with it for close to an hour, turning it outside in and inside out, while every mosquito and no-see-um in the whole of Passamaquoddy Bay made a meal of my tender western skin. Defeated, I crawled into the front seat of the compact car to itch for a few sleepless hours, leaving Bernie's tent puddled on the ground.

Maybe this trip to revisit old camping grounds was a mistake, I thought. But in the morning I saw a silver lining emerge from the clouds of insects that had made my night miserable, for only a couple of miles down the road, a tiny tributary stream made a seam in a lake where my father and I had caught landlocked salmon 35 years before. Spotting that stream was like finding a jewel buried on a map marked by an X. I waded as far into the cool water as my waist, until I was no taller than the child who had stood on the shore and held a rod that thumped with the gleaming turns of a fish that was bigger than any he had ever caught before.

On the chance that your experience with uncooperative tents will not be redeemed by such a happy ending, take the time to become familiar with their idiosyncrasies at home first. The same goes for camp stoves, lanterns, generators, or any other piece of equipment that might not prove as simple to operate as the instructions suggest.

ARRIVING AT CAMP

Unless you have a reservation, the best time to arrive in camp is midmorning, when campers who have been packing up shop are getting ready to leave. Some campgrounds will fill up before noon, others not at all; but as a rule of thumb, you'll have more open spaces to choose from between 9 A.M. and 11 A.M. than at any other time.

Often when we have been packing camp, another family will stop and ask if they can have our space when we leave. This is a common campground practice and should not be considered an imposition.

When you arrive at a popular campground, it's a good idea to drop someone off at the first decent open site you find. Then you can drive the campground loops to try to find a better place without worrying that a car following you will take the last open site. Pack a couple of lawn chairs where they are easy to get at, then drop them off to hold the site before going back to the entrance to pay.

PICKING A CAMPSITE

Selecting a campsite is dependent upon any number of factors, perhaps the most important being the lay of the land. A tent pitched over top of hard roots and rocks is not going to afford you much rest, and one pitched in a depression will float away with an onslaught of rain.

The ideal campsite is on high ground that is soft enough to drive a stake into and has enough flat ground to pitch your tent. It should have some shade from the midday sun and a few natural windbreaks such as trees or large boulders, yet be situated to capture enough of a breeze to keep flying insects from making your life miserable. Your campsite should be fairly

It is mighty hard to resist setting up camp by a beautiful lake or stream. But remember, you'll have to watch the children more closely, and mosquitoes may be more of a problem.

close to both the water spigot and the bathroom but upwind of the outhouse. It should have a well-ventilated fire ring with enough flat ground around it to set up a few chairs. The ideal site should also have good spacing from neighbors and be far away from the generator hum of motorhomes or other RVs.

Most campers prefer lakeside or riverbank sites to those set far back into the trees, but those aren't always the best spots for families that include small children. Toddlers who are naturally inquisitive can seldom be left out of their parents' sight under the best of circumstances. You would never think of camping with them next to the lip of a cliff, yet some people don't pause to consider that having a deep, swift-flowing river in front of camp is almost as dangerous. That's one reason to forgo rivers and camp near shallow streams or lakes until children become older, although you can never drop your guard entirely, for it is just as easy to drown in a few inches of water as a few feet of it.

Also, boggy or weedy sites near the water's edge will be buggier than those set on a bench a few feet higher and farther back. The dew line (or in fall, the frost line) embraces the banks of a stream or river for some little distance, and those who pitch camp inside the perimeter will wake up with their tents dripping wet and their shoes only temporarily dry. And keep in mind that it can be 10 to 15 degrees colder in the river bottom than on a high bank overlooking it.

If you have grandparents in camp, try to pick sites that have no exposed roots or other obstacles and which are close to smooth, wide paths leading to the bathroom. When pitching tents and erecting rain flies, be careful not to position guy ropes where they could be tripped over by someone moving about after dark. What to you or me is a painful fall could mean a broken hip for them.

Usually the most coveted sites are those that offer the most privacy. Often they are located at the very edge of the campground, closest to the woods. But in wilderness camps, it is just such sites that are most likely to be visited by bears and mountain lions. This is nothing to become paranoid over, but in a few areas the chances of encountering an unwanted prowler may be high enough to tip the pendulum in favor of a site that's closer to company.

PITCHING THE TENT

The Plains Indians customarily faced the openings in their tepees to the east, to capture the first rays of the sun. Campers who have been up staring at embers or talking late into the night may not feel the same imperative. To me, it seems natural to place the doorway either toward the water or a striking vista. However, if you are camping in a dusty area or near the ocean's blowing sands, pitch your tent with the door opening facing away from the prevailing winds.

Pick up any sticks or rocks from the tent site, then spread out your ground cloth. Ground cloths (any kind of heavy, plastic or water-

---

Pre-selected Campsites

Everybody likes to select his or her own campsite. But more and more often when you visit a state or national park, a uniformed employee will greet you at the gate to the campground and assign one to you. From the park's standpoint, this policy lends organization and efficiency to what had previously been a laissez-faire, first-come, first-served operation. Plus it gets campers to pay upon entering, rather than waiting their own sweet time, and sometimes having to be goaded by personnel carrying a clipboard the next morning.

For campers, such a preemptive strike renders the pioneer, find-your-home-in-the-wilderness aspect of camping moot, and can make the experience just a little bit more like checking into a motel.

The obvious way around this problem is to avoid these campgrounds. Nonetheless, our family has had many enjoyable camping trips in just such places, and we have picked up a few tips for getting a good site. If you are familiar with the campground, request a loop or section that you would prefer and tell the attendant. If you don't like the site selected for you, it's sometimes productive to request another, much better one that you have found open nearby. A genuine smile and a good attitude may be able to persuade the employee to alter your site. Remember, the person at the gate is not the one who made the policy, so treat him or her courteously.

Another strategy my wife and I have employed is to make a list of several good campsites for future reference; that way, if we ever return to the campground, we can ask whether any of those sites are available.

resistant cloth will do; the grommeted poly tarps sold in hardware stores are cheap and work very well) serve two purposes—to keep the floor of the tent dry in rainy weather and to preserve the material from dirt, mildew, and abrasion. Fold the cloth to the size of the tent floor and tuck in exposed edges to keep rain from accumulating between the two layers of fabric.

Before staking down the corners of the tent, lie down on it to make certain the site you have chosen is as flat as it looks. If there is a little slope to the ground (and there almost always is) pitch your tent with the back end slightly elevated for your head. Most campers like to sleep with their heads toward the back, because the floor area inside the door is more likely to get wet and dirty from foot traffic.

Erecting the Rain Fly

The decision to put up a rain fly depends on how much gambling blood runs through your veins. The odds are that if you do put up a fly it won't rain, you'll have shade where you wanted the sun, the fly will come crashing down in the wind, and someone will utter curses after tripping over the

---

Securing Your Foundation

Even high quality tents often come with cheap aluminum stakes that bend out of shape under hammering, or cheap plastic stakes that soon break. For a pittance you can buy stout ABS plastic stakes (standard accessories with L.L. Bean's larger tents) or Army surplus metal stakes that work much better.

A few do's and dont's:

- Do stake down the corners first, but don't stretch the tent floor drum tight.
- Do drive stakes straight down or angled slightly toward the tent. Don't slant stakes away from the tent.
- Don't bury the heads of stakes in hard ground. It will be difficult to pry them back up.
- Don't attempt to pull up stuck stakes by yanking on the loops sewn to the tent floor. You will damage your tent.
- Do pull up stuck stakes by inserting the claw of a hammer or back edge of a hatchet and prying them out.
- When camping on very hard ground, do consider alternatives. Hold down tent loops and corners with smooth rocks or tie to logs.
- Do bring extra stakes in case one is lost or broken.

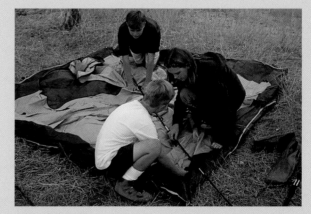

For children, there's magic in putting up a tent. Stout stakes and outside clips for the tent poles make the job easier.

guy ropes. And if you don't put up a fly it most certainly will rain, the children will sit in the car with misery written on their faces, and someone trying to store the gear before it gets soaked will call down curses on the heavens.

This dome tent is almost up, but the children's job isn't done yet. They'll need to secure the rain fly over the top before crawling inside. It takes a few minutes more work, but it is easier than scrambling to do it in the middle of a dark, rainy night.

For many years, we erred on the safe side and put a tarp up over the picnic table as a matter of habit during longer trips. But I got tired of ducking my head to step underneath and my neck got sore from the posture I assumed over the cookstove, because the edge of the tarp was close enough to the end of the table that I couldn't stand up straight. And sometimes it was too dark under there to see what I was doing.

Innovative rain-fly designs offered by L.L. Bean and other makers eliminate some of the problems associated with conventional flies (for a discussion of rain-fly types, see Chapter 9), but they still get in the way and make pitching and striking camp take a little longer.

Now we use prayer to push the clouds away and keep the fly lashed to the roof rack in case that doesn't work.

ESTABLISHING CAMP BOUNDARIES

Camping shouldn't be all work, but the bookend parts of it, the setting up and tearing down, certainly are. Children who arrive in camp will be desperate to jump out of the car and take off running. If you are uncomfortable letting them out of sight, but can't keep an eye on them while the tent is giving you fits, establish clearly marked boundaries—this tree, that garbage can, the blue Ford—and explain to them that for the next few minutes you will be very busy and they must stay within those markers. After they have run off a little steam, get them involved in helping out around camp.

SHARING CAMPGROUND CHORES

In the rush to set up camp and make a vacation run efficiently, don't overlook the willingness of children to pitch in and help. Remember, they are natural campers, having set up their

Children can sleep just about anywhere, especially after helping to set up camp.

own makeshift tents out of blankets in their bedrooms since before kindergarten. There is no reason they can't do the same in the woods.

Trolling through nearby campsites for firewood, helping to pitch the tent, pounding stakes with a hammer (never a hatchet), and arranging the pads and sleeping bags are among the chores first and second graders can start helping with. For me, fetching water brings back special memories: leaning on the green-painted pump handle with both hands until the water flowed, awkwardly trying to balance a water jug under the gushing stream, and never getting more than a couple of cups full before the pressure dropped. Today, conventional water spigots have replaced pump handles in all but a treasured handful of campgrounds, rendering the adventure of fetching water into the simplest of chores, albeit one that still manages to get most kids' feet wet.

Kids can also help with food preparation, setting the picnic table, and cleaning up after dinner. Our kids like going on a hunt for stones to weigh down napkins so they don't blow away in the wind.

Supervise children around cookstoves and lanterns. My nephew, Elliott, severely burned the palm of his hand when he picked up a lantern by its hot wire handle. The handle was hot because it was folded against the side, rather than upright, but he shouldn't have touched it in either case. Keep children away from all gear that generates heat until they are mature enough to be trusted. The same goes for hatchets and axes.

CAMPING WITH PETS

Having camped with cats and dogs since I was a child, it has become clear to me that the decision to bring pets along depends less on the nature of the trip than it does on the nature of the individual animal. We had an easy-going Siamese who tucked her paws under her chest and started to purr as soon as my father turned the key to the car engine. In camp she would

*Many people consider their pets part of the family. Taking them along can be work,
but it cuts kennel costs and can add to the pleasure of the trip.*

curl up in my mother's lap and otherwise was content to explore the perimeter of her leash
and make short dashes to catch mice after dark. Our friends Bob and Duncan Bullock
camped with an old golden retriever who slept between their children, helping to warm them
on autumn nights, and never needed a leash as long as she lived.

At the other end of spectrum are cats that are terrified of the car, try to escape the moment
a door is opened, and make every possible attempt to hang themselves on their collars by
straining at the leash. Barking dogs that chase animals and snarl at passing children should
never be taken camping.

Be aware that most campgrounds have leash laws. Follow the rules out of consideration for
other campers and wild animals. A few campgrounds do not permit pets, so call ahead to
check the regulations.

If you do decide to take your pet camping, here are a few tips to keep in mind:

- Don't feed pets just before the trip; it can make them more nervous. Your veterinarian
  can provide mild tranquilizers for temperamental travelers.
- Stop every hour or so to exercise dogs and let them go to the bathroom. Make kitty litter
  available for traveling cats and keep a paper plate handy in case your pet acts like it's going to throw up.
- Because trips are stressful to your pet, don't vary its diet.
- For cats, make a leash of thin, strong cord which can be tied to a stake in camp. Tether
  cats on open ground, where the cord can't become tangled in camp chairs, on picnic

tables, or around tree trunks. A tangled cord can lead to serious injuries. You can make a run for cats or dogs by stretching an overhead cord between two trees and looping the leash handle through the end.

- Bring all pets inside the tent or camper at night.

- If you are planning to cross the Canadian border, make certain you have up-to-date records of rabies vaccinations. You will be turned back if you don't, which happened to us once at the border between Glacier Park in Montana and Waterton Park in Alberta.

- Be careful about leaving pets in cars on hot days. Even with the windows cracked, temperatures can soar well above 100°F.

- Make certain your pet has a collar with your name, address, and phone number clearly written. Twice, my parents have lost cats that sneaked out of the vehicle, but both times they were fortunate enough to find them the next day. Keep a photo of your pet in the glove compartment to help people identify it.

- If your dog or cat sleeps on a favorite blanket or in a special basket at home, bring it on the trip. It will make the transition go more smoothly.

- Never leave pets unattended in camp, unless they are securely locked inside a trailer or motorhome.

CAMPGROUND PESTS

Small animals such as porcupines, raccoons, squirrels, and mice, as well as crows, blue jays, and the ubiquitous gray jay (appropriately nicknamed the camp robber), become pests only if you encourage them by leaving food outside when the campsite is unattended. Even skunks are no cause for alarm, as long as you don't have a dog or make any sudden movements to scare them. Cade's Cove Campground in Great Smoky Mountains National Park in Tennessee used to play host to dozens of gorgeous, double-lined skunks that wandered underneath our camp chairs when I was a boy.

We fed them, as did most campers in those more innocent times. Today, I stress to my children that feeding camp visitors is unwise, because animals that become dependent on handouts are less likely to survive during harsh winters than those which remain wild, and are more likely to be destroyed when they become too much of a nuisance.

Insects can and will get into food boxes if they are left unattended for long periods of time. Make a habit of keeping boxes and coolers up off the ground during meal times and store them away in the car or trailer the rest of the day.

CAMPGROUND ETIQUETTE

Noisy human neighbors can be much more of a camp nuisance than the wild ones with black noses and four feet. The most common offenders include people who run noisy generators late into the night and play loud music. Most campers will quiet down if asked politely, but unfortunately there are exceptions. If neighbors persist in being obnoxious, short of an ugly confrontation, about all you can do is move camp or report the behavior to the campground host or a ranger, if one is present.

Many campgrounds post quiet hours. Generally speaking, state and national park campgrounds, as well as forest campgrounds that have live-in hosts, are better at keeping noise under control than unsupervised camps near towns, where teens gather to party.

Drivers who speed on campground loops pose a more serious threat to safety. Remember that camping is a family affair and children will be walking, playing, and riding bicycles without giving much thought to traffic. Speed bumps have been installed on many campground roads; I wish there were more of them.

THE DIRTY TRUTH ABOUT CAMPING

It gets to some people sooner than others, the oily hair and itching scalp, the shirt that reeks of wood smoke and mosquito repellent, the sticky sweat and clammy feel of skin while you wait for sleep to lay your thoughts to rest. If you are hunting or fishing hard, or backpacking a dozen miles every day, you're generally too tired to notice and your companions are in no position to throw the first stone.

But in a family camp, a reasonable degree of cleanliness matters. Some private and state park campgrounds provide coin-operated showers, making the task of washing up simple. We had no such conveniences in the Michigan campgrounds I lived in during my youth, and I can remember my mother painstakingly heating pot after pot of water on the Coleman stove and scrubbing our heads while my brother and I squeezed our eyes shut. Sponge baths inside the tent, standing on a towel, were just as dreadful, leaving a skim of soap on the skin that made me itch.

Many campers can get by swimming every other day and washing up a couple times a week with heated water and biodegradable soap. Adults also can do a bang up job by gritting their teeth against the cold and washing under the spigot with soap and a handkerchief before neighboring campers are awake. But be careful when holding your head under very cold water not to get it into your ears; it can give you an earache that lasts for hours.

Kids are understandably less tolerant of freezing water and most I've been associated with make it plain that they don't see the need for washing in the first place. They have a point. Pre-adolescents don't sweat much and can usually get by for a few days without a bath, as long as you keep their hands clean and wash their faces daily. Disposable moist towelettes make cleaning up simple and should be a staple on every family camping trip.

Fastidious teenagers or adults who are desperate for a shower can usually find one with a little looking. My sister-in-law, Linda McCafferty, has been known to drive 40 miles from camp in search of showers and has ferreted them out in motels (for a small fee), youth hostels, public swimming pools, truck stops, and, of course, coin laundries. The campground host or booth attendant will be a good source of local information.

Portable camp showers are an option I wouldn't have recommended a few years ago, because the sun showers I tried never heated the water. However, there are a variety of better designs now on the market, including one that heats water by thermal siphoning. Copper coils are heated either on a stove burner or in a fire and conduct heat to the water container. You can buy a shower stall or rig one with an extra tarp or a couple of rain ponchos.

BATHROOMS

Bathrooms are the bane of the camping experience for some people, especially newcomers to the outdoors. Pit toilets are indeed the pits, but they can be made considerably more tolerable with air-freshener packets and quality toilet paper.

Portable toilets are an option, especially for children who are being toilet trained and might not make it to the outhouse in time. They range from simple seats that use garbage bags for disposal, to models with removable liner buckets, through more expensive seats that have detachable water chambers and bellows pumps that can be flushed dozens of times before emptying. Most are bulky affairs that take up considerable cargo space, which is a problem with the more elaborate portable shower systems, too.

The practical solution is to vacation in campgrounds that have a level of plumbing sophistication everyone can endure, or invest in a tent trailer or small motorhome that has its own bathroom. Save more primitive trips for like-minded companions, which will include your children if you start camping with them early in their lives.

NO-TRACE CAMPING

Leaving no trace in the wilderness is a skill every camper should practice and pass onto his or her children. In many backcountry areas, that means no fires, no alteration of the campsite, no camping within 200 feet of the bank of a stream or the shoreline of a lake, burying human waste, and packing out of all garbage, including toilet paper. Even biodegradable soap is too harsh for fragile environments.

In developed campgrounds, it means leaving the site in better shape than you found it. Through continued use, most campsites will show some erosion around the picnic table and fire ring, as well as one or two flat areas where previous tenants have pitched their tents. Use the flattened areas for your own tent; don't pitch it on top of the remaining vegetation. Use only downed, dead timber for campfires. Collect wood well away from the camp-ground, so as not to contribute to de-nuding the forest floor in camp. Don't scatter firewood coals when you pull camp; either burn them completely or leave them for the next camper. Bag ashes and dump them in a garbage can. And definitely do not put nails in tree trunks.

Except on sandy beaches, digging rain trenches around tent sites can leave scars on the earth that may not heal for years. If you use a ground cloth and se-lect a site with good drainage, trenching isn't necessary.

Minimize impact by building small

Caring for the local environment means sus-taining the land for generations to come.

fires and keeping a neat camp. Having slept first in a tiny tent, and subsequently in larger tents, a trailer, tent trailer, motorhome and mini-motorhome, I have come full circle in forty years and am back to keeping my camp as unobtrusive as possible. A tent, a table, a few chairs, a hammock for my daughter, and a rain fly that stays packed until it rains; that's it.

Each piece of gear we bring to the woods distances us just a little bit more from nature. Be-sides, the smaller the camp, the easier it is to pack up and be on your way.

PULLING STAKES

Strike camp in the reverse order it was pitched, by first organizing all the cooking gear and food, rolling up the hammock, packing the lantern into its case, airing out sleeping bags, and dragging all personal items and sleeping pads out of the tent. Get the children to pitch in; it's not only good training but makes the process go a lot faster. If you are leaving in the morning, let the tent stand while you pack the other gear so that the dew can dry. Then turn it floor-side up for the bottom to dry. If you haven't used a ground cloth, wipe all the pine needles and dirt off the bottom with a broom or paper towels. Many times you will have no choice but to put the tent away wet; just be sure to air dry it at home before placing it in storage, in order to prevent mildew. Canvas tents put away wet can be ruined by rot.

Every camper soon discovers that no matter how tightly the tent is rolled, it will not fit into the stuff sack you brought it in. This is a rule to which I have found no exceptions, and I have owned a lot of tents. One trick is to roll the tent longer than the sack, and thereby a little thinner. The end will hang out a little, but at least you'll be able to get most of it into the sack. Another solution is to separate the tent and the poles, stuff the tent into the sack, and use a couple of bungee cords to lash the poles to it.

If you are moving from camp to camp with a cabin-style tent,

The Camp Repair Kit

Quality camping gear usually needs little upkeep. However, it's always a good idea to pack a simple repair kit for emergencies. Here are a few suggestions:

- Duct tape (for patching holes in tent, leaky seams, etc.)
- Heavy-duty needle and thread (dental floss is a strong, all-purpose camp thread) for sewing rips in tent fabric, backpacks, etc.
- Safety pins
- Pole sleeve for repairing broken tent or rain-fly poles
- Small hose clamps for splinting broken tent poles
- Strong nylon cord (550 cord sold in camping stores and Army-Navy outlets is the best) for tying rain tarps to trees, replacing boot laces in an emergency, etc.
- Rubber cement and patch kit for repairing leaks in inflatable mattresses (sold in sporting goods stores)

On trips where you camp far from towns, it's a good idea to add to the list an extra globe for your lantern and replacement generators for fuel lanterns or camp stoves. A knife hone and a file to sharpen ax blades also come in handy on extended trips.

it's simpler just to tape the aluminum poles together and tie them to the roof rack. Do the same with the poles for the rain fly. It will make the process of pitching and pulling camp go a lot faster.

After the car is packed, have a last look around to check for anything you or the children may have left behind. It's better to take a minute to do this than to drive 40 miles back to the campground after it dawns on you that your knife is no longer in your pocket or that your fly rod is still leaning against the tree. And while you're at it, pick up bits of paper and any cigarette butts that may have been flipped onto the ground. The future of camping, of all outdoor recreation, depends in large part upon how conscientious we are about leaving the earth as we found it.

CHAPTER
5

Camp Cooking

"Hunger is the best sauce."
ANCIENT PROVERB

When I was growing up, camp cooking was the domain of my father, a man whose idea of *haute cuisine* stopped at good ground round. Our meals veered sharply toward the Spartan. If Dad had caught trout the night before, breakfasts were fish fried in the same skillet with diced potatoes that had been boiled the night before and chilled in the cooler overnight. Dinners were cooked with the same economy of gesture. On one memorable occasion, the main course consisted of steaks laid directly onto the campfire coals and slapped down on a paper plate with a paper towel to wipe off the ash. Buffalo steaks, Dad called them, and once you got past the grit, they weren't half bad.

In fact, all of his meals were good, if a mite too austere for some people's tastes. And his kitchen was a model of efficiency that obeyed the five rules every camp cook should take to heart.

Rule #1: Pack only what you need.

Nearly every novice takes too much of two things—clothes and food. The best way I've found to keep grub to a minimum is to make a list. If my wife and children and I are going to camp for two nights, then we're going to need two camp breakfasts, three lunches, and two dinners. I pack accordingly. That means if I plan a scrambled egg breakfast the second morning, I pack six eggs—I don't take the full dozen. This sounds simple enough, but you'd be surprised how many campers make the mistake of waiting until the last minute, then rushing to the grocery store and stacking boxes into the car.

Rule # 2: Pre-cook and pre-mix whenever possible.

My father's trout breakfasts would have taken more than twice as long to prepare had he not cooked the potatoes beforehand. Rice and pasta also can be pre-cooked, refrigerated in reclosable freezer bags, and heated back up in camp. Just dump the pasta into a pot of hot water for a couple of minutes. (No, it won't be *al dente,* but would you rather listen to children complain for half an hour while waiting for water to boil?) Rice can be reheated by immersing the plastic bag in hot (not boiling) water, or heated right in the pan with stir-fry or Cajun dishes.

Another trick I've learned is to make a double batch of more complicated dishes such as Creole chicken at home, then freeze

Campers don't have to forgo a comfortable eating arrangement just because space in the car is limited. Such companies as L.L. Bean offer lightweight but sturdy tables and chairs that pack up compactly and are easily assembled.

the appropriate amount of leftovers for a camp meal. Sealed in a freezer bag, they will keep quite well for a couple of months and have the added advantage of cooling other perishable food in the ice chest.

You can also shortcut cooking times by pre-mixing at home. For example, I combine the dry ingredients for biscuit mix and seal them in a plastic bag along with the recipe, jotted down on a slip of paper. That way, all that's left to do in camp is heat up the Dutch oven, cut in the right amount of margarine, and add buttermilk before kneading the dough.

Rule # 3: Use nature's bounty when ecologically sound.

"A trout is too valuable to catch only once." Famed angler Lee Wulff summarized the catch-and-release philosophy in this country with those words, with the result that today many anglers regard killing any fish as nothing short of an ecological disaster. What some people don't understand is that Wulff's concern was for the diminishing stocks of wild trout in rivers like Montana's Madison, which are subject to tremendous angling pressure and are not, nor should they be, periodically replenished with truckloads of hatchery fish.

By contrast, the vast majority of camping is done on the shores of small streams, mountain lakes, or reservoirs where killing a few sunfish, crappies, or small trout does the fishery little harm. In fact, many of the alpine lakes that offer the most pristine camping are historically sterile and have no natural reproduction; their fisheries are strictly put and take. Other lakes and streams have been stocked with brook trout or bluegills, species that tend to overpopulate and stunt unless they are harvested.

Fresh-caught fish are delicious. Catching, cleaning, and cooking them offers children insight into the pyramid of nature—little fish eat insect larvae, big fish eat little fish, people eat

Fishing for dinner can be great fun. It also can offer a child insight into the pyramid of nature.

the big fish—that they simply cannot get by consuming halibut steaks plastic-wrapped by the grocer. I always plan at least one fish dinner a week on camping trips, along with a meal of venison if there's any left in the freezer. Oyster and morel mushrooms, watercress, cattails, berries, and wild onions have made the menu as well.

Rule # 4: Dirty as few dishes as possible.

Because cooking ought to be one of the greatest enjoyments of camp life, I lean to the unnecessary and create more work for myself than is absolutely necessary. For example, venison or beef steaks marinated in a homemade teriyaki, or grilled mallard, or chicken breasts can stand quite well on their own You really don't have to dirty an extra pot with a packaged Béarnaise or port wine/currant jelly sauce. But that extra touch is the difference between eating and dining, like the flowers my wife cuts in her garden and carries in the cooler to brighten the picnic table. (My father's camp table, needless to say, was not adorned with flowers.) Still, I have yet to undertake a meal, gourmet or otherwise, that couldn't be conquered with a couple skillets, a sheet of tin foil, and a medium pot.

Rule # 5: Keep cleanup simple.

In camp, paper plates are always the order of the day. Although our family's cookbox contains a plastic bottle of liquid nondetergent soap and a small scrub sponge for dish washing, the truth is we seldom use either. Even biodegradable soap is too harsh for fragile environments and it really isn't needed. I just set it on the table for show once in a while to pacify guests.

Instead, when dinner starts to wind down, I pump up the stove and light both burners. On one I place a pot of water, on the other the dirty skillet that has been swabbed out with a paper towel until it is fairly clean. As each person finishes, he or she drops a dirty paper plate into a plastic trash bag underneath the edge of the table and places the dirty forks, spoons, and cooking utensils into the skillet of simmering water. By the time the pot boils, the utensils have been sterilized. While they cool, either my wife or I will clean the drinking cups with the clean hot water in the pot. Then we empty the skillet water. In developed campgrounds (like the ones in most national parks), you can dump wash water in a wastewater disposal commode; in more primitive camps, it's okay to scatter the water on the ground, as long as the food particles have been swabbed out first. After the clean utensils and dishes are

Cooking with Children

For many children, roasting marshmallows and hot dogs over the fire will be their first experience at heating food. You can buy metal roasting sticks at camping supply stores or whittle sticks from green wood. I prefer the latter. Whittling teaches children something about tool making and making do with the gifts of nature. It can serve as a supervised introduction to working with a knife, stressing the basics, such as pushing the cutting edge of the blade away from you. My son was seven when he was first permitted to use a knife under supervision. Just be careful to use either a fixed blade or a folding knife that locks open, because any child's first attempts will be awkward and the blade of an ordinary folding knife could close on his or her fingers. And don't mar campsites by cutting limbs from living shrubs or trees. Instead, use shoots from streambank willows that have been uprooted or the suckers reaching from tree limbs that have fallen in the forest.

Pie-irons (RV supply stores sell them as "camp cookers") consist of two hinged metal plates attached to long metal rods with wooden handles. They are designed to sandwich two slices of bread with a filling in between. Placed over the coals and turned to evenly brown both pieces of bread, they bake superb pizzas and pies. When I was a child, I eagerly looked forward to the night we could each make our own pizzas. This is a tradition Gail and I have passed down to our children, who are no less enthusiastic.

To make a pie-iron pizza, spread a little margarine or butter on one side of two pieces of bread. Open the pie-iron and press the buttered side of one slice of bread against the inside of the metal plate. If the slice doesn't quite fit, you can either cut it or force the edges to conform to the proper shape. Then sprinkle the bread with mozzarella cheese, drizzle pizza sauce over it, and add pepperoni or any other topping you choose. Lay the second slice over the filling and bring the halves together. The cookers come with a little clasp to keep the halves from accidentally separating.

The trick to cooking with a pie-iron is not burning the bread. You'll have to keep an eye on the kids and remind them to open up the cooker once every couple minutes to check the progress.

Two suggestions: Always buy the square instead of the round-shaped cookers. They're not only bigger, you also won't waste bread by cutting around the edges. Pie-irons are inexpensive, so buy two and dinner will get done twice as fast.

Our family often schedules pie-iron pizzas for a night when we won't get back to camp before dark, because there is so little preparation or cleanup involved. After the pizzas are cooked, we wipe off the pie-irons, add new slices of bread, and fill them with a few tablespoons of blueberry or cherry pie filling. The baked pies make a great kids' dessert.

For many children, roasting marshmallows and hot dogs over the fire will be their first experience at cooking their own food.

Cooking with pie-irons over a campfire is a wonderful way to turn an ordinary sandwich into outdoor-style pizza. Kids love it!

dried with a dish towel, the sponge makes its first and only appearance—to wipe down the tablecloth.

I don't bother cleaning the outside of pots blackened by fire. In order to keep them clean, you can coat the exterior with dishwashing liquid before putting them on the fire, but once blackened, the pots hesat much faster and it's a simple matter to place them in a plastic or paper bag to keep other dishes from getting dirtied.

BREAKFAST

For the cook, dawn is easily the most peaceful time of the day. Slipping out of the tent and buttoning up an old wool shirt; gathering sticks to rekindle the fire; fueling it with wood chunks split the night before, so the sound of the ax won't wake up the children; laying out a breakfast of bacon, brook trout, and Dutch oven biscuits before anyone else begins to stir; then settling near the fire to greet sunrise with a cup of cowboy coffee—now there is a portrait of American camping that Norman Rockwell should have immortalized in oils.

It's also an image he might have had to get out of his sleeping bag a few mornings to find. We aren't the same people that Rockwell brushstroked to life on calendars back in the 1930s. Americans are more in a hurry to get somewhere now: to be first on the trout stream, to be first on the trail, to be first on the road to wherever it is we think we have to be next. Although I still strive to schedule a few layover days in camp, and believe with all my heart that the smell of bacon frying in an iron skillet is not only one of life's quintessential sensory pleasures but that cholesterol eaten outdoors doesn't count, the fact is that the pulse of my own family is not too far behind the national pace.

Pancakes offer a first step in scaling back the size of breakfast. Use a mix that needs only water to make the batter (Krusteaz's Honey Whole Wheat is our favorite). Set the syrup bottle in a pot of hot water and use the nonstick skillet from the cookbox. Add a sprinkling of semi-sweet chocolate chips to the batter and you can count on the kids starting the day with a good attitude.

New York-style bagels that are lightly toasted on the grill make a simple, refined breakfast. They will keep for several days if stored cold, but beware of the garlic bagels—they will quickly cause the cooler to reek. On mornings when breakfast has to be reduced to a bite and a gulp, a paper bowl of granola or cereal and milk is a proven quick fix.

Ardent animal watchers often have to be up before dawn and won't want to take any time to eat. For example, if you want your children to see the wolves that roam the Lamar Valley in Yellowstone National Park, you'll have to hit road by 5 A.M. Zucchini or banana bread sandwiches with cream cheese filling, accompanied by canned juice, cantaloupe slices stored in a plastic container, and a Thermos of coffee, provide a filling meal that can be eaten on the road. It just takes a few minutes the night before to prepare the breakfast, stick it in the cooler, and fill the Thermos with cocoa or coffee.

LUNCH

Keep it simple, keep it light, and above all, let it be cold. Camping is work enough without having to cook and wash dishes three times a day.

Peanut butter or lunch meat sandwiches, juices, cookies, and fruit are standard fare. A French baguette and a couple of good cheeses make an elegant change of pace. For that matter, there is nothing wrong with spreading a checked cloth on the riverbank, breaking open a bottle of white wine, and adding a cold grouse breast or pâté to the menu, except that you'll have to prepare a second lunch for the kids.

Our family seems to be always on the go at midday, usually miles from the campground, so whatever we eat for lunch has to be packed in the car or the backpacks. Pack along a box of small plastic bags for trail lunches. You'll find you go through quite a few of them and that they have many other uses as well.

DINNER

Probably the cardinal sin of campground cooking is waiting until dark to start dinner. Not only do children become cranky without food, but even the simplest task grows exponentially more difficult after the sun sets. Lantern light has many fine qualities—setting

---

Trail Foods

Nearly all groceries, even the mom-and-pop operations in north woods backwaters, carry a good selection of granola, trail mixes, peanuts, chocolate bars, graham crackers, and other snack foods.

Jerky is one traditional favorite that can be improved on by making it yourself. I like to use venison or turkey breast, because neither is laced with fat the way beef can be. To make jerky, slice meat with the grain into strips no more than ⅜-inch thick and an inch or two wide. The best all-around marinade and basting sauce I've found comes from the kitchen of my sister-in-law, Linda McCafferty (see recipe on p. 68). Marinate turkey, beef, or venison strips overnight in the refrigerator. Dry the meat with paper towels, then rub in cracked peppercorns or extra salt to taste.

If you don't have a smoker, jerky can be prepared in a conventional oven. Drape strips on cake cooling racks and place the cake racks on your oven racks, first lining the bottom of the oven with tin foil to catch drips. Set temperature to 150°F and crack the door with a pencil. Depending on the thickness of the strips, the jerky should be done in six to 10 hours. To test, bend a slice with your fingers. It should be pliable, just verging on cracking. Cool. Refrigerate or freeze until use.

Many intrepid backpackers use a dehydrator to dry their own apple slices, apricots, and peaches. Dried fruits can be rather expensive to buy processed, but are worth it if you need to keep weight down in your pack. For day hiking, regular lunch foods won't be too heavy to pack.

a mood for romance, for example—but it is *not* an adequate substitute for natural light to cook by.

If you start early enough, you can duplicate just about any meal you would enjoy at home in camp. I once cooked an extravagant moose bourguignon from scratch, slaving over the Coleman stove for hours, but it's a better idea to prepare complicated dishes at home and freeze the leftovers for camp. Even elaborate seafood dishes, such as shrimp étouffée, can be cooked at home and frozen, minus the shrimp. After three or four days of camping, find a pay shower, clean up, buy a pound of shrimp, and treat yourself to an elegant candlelight dinner, minus the work. But make sure these dishes are favorites of the children, too. Camp cooking is too much of a hardship if you have to prepare a second meal for the kids.

Spaghetti is standard camp fare and takes little time to prepare if you use fresh pasta or dried pasta that has been pre-cooked at home. If you plan on cooking dried pasta in camp, choose angel hair, which is very thin and cooks quickly. Don't overlook such simple dishes as hot dogs, burgers, and beans. A child with a cooking stick in his hand and a hot dog sizzling over the fire is a happy child. And don't forget a couple of big cans of soup for evenings when it's pouring rain or you get back to camp too late to feel like cooking.

COOKING METHODS

Cooking with Camp Stoves

Cooking on a camp stove is an exercise in juggling. Dishes that need boiling water or high heat should be cooked on the burner with the higher BTU output, which is the one closest to the fuel source and capable of producing a hotter flame (some newer stoves produce equal heat output with both burners). Once a dish is cooking, it can be transferred to the second burner while another dish is started on the main ring. If you need a third pot, place a lid or sheet of tin foil over a dish that is mostly cooked and keep it warm next to the campfire.

Cooking takes longer in camp than it does at home. Food preparation is a little more complicated, because you are working with camp utensils and sometimes using a paper plate as a cutting board. With most stoves, it takes longer to bring water to a boil and at high elevations, the water boils at a lower temperature, which adds to the cooking time. Because the burner rings on most stoves are small, you will need to move skillets and pots side to side to heat the bottoms evenly. In cool weather, cooked dishes will lose heat rapidly, so it's important to reheat all dishes quickly just before serving.

The key is patience. Start meals early. Until you gain experience, keep to one-pot meals and other uncomplicated dishes. And don't leave your stove unattended. Stove valves that are partly clogged by fuel residue tend to flare up and recede, flare up and recede (again, not so much of a problem with newer stoves). Never take the heat output for granted, because it can and will change at any time.

On the plus side, food cooked outdoors and served to hungry campers smells and tastes better than it would indoors, even if it isn't perfectly presented.

Cooking with Fire

It's difficult to resist the temptation to grill meats over an open fire, but until you have mastered the technique, probably the best advice anyone can give you is to pack an extra

Cooking on a camp stove can be an exercise in juggling. A good utility box like this one, sold by L.L. Bean, makes a great outdoor kitchen.

steak or chicken breast to replace the one that will turn to cinder while you try to fish it out of the flames.

The biggest mistakes most people make when grilling are 1) not building the fire large enough and soon enough to create a bed of coals with which to cook, 2) attempting to grill over the fire itself instead of over hot coals that have been pulled to the side, and 3) the technique that is fraught with disaster—using a grill that is either too small, too flimsy, or too precariously balanced.

A sturdy rectangular grill at least 20 inches long and almost as wide is perfect, and shouldn't cost more than a few dollars. Sporting goods stores sell grills as well as grilling baskets that close with long handles and securely hold burgers, steaks, or fish. In a pinch, you can make do with the grill from your backyard barbecue. To keep your grill from dirtying up the back of the car and other gear, store it in a large plastic trash bag or a makeshift envelope of cardboard cut from a box.

Back in the days of stone campfire rings, it was a simple matter to rearrange the stones to make a small rectangular cooking area adjacent to the main fire. As coals were needed for grilling, they were shoveled from the fire into the rectangular area. The cooking was done well away from the flames, the grill was sturdily supported on three sides by stones, the steaks sizzled without catching fire, and one could imagine gods of medieval gluttony writhing in the flames.

This design, known as a keyhole fire, is still the best for serious grilling, but stone fire rings have gone the way of cavemen in many campgrounds. Too many people abused camping privileges by building additional fire rings, until some campsites came to resemble the Olympic insignia. Today, most campgrounds have fireplaces in one of two designs: either a half-barrel that is buried in the ground, or a grate that resembles an upside-down cardboard box with thick iron crossbars across the top. The latter are worthless for grilling and those with solid sides have next to no air circulation, making them pretty poor fireplaces to boot. About all one can do is scrape a few coals just outside the mouth of the grate, set up a couple of stones to prop the grill on, and cook just beyond the letter of the law. (Most campgrounds having stipulations against cooking outside the grate.) I'll admit I've done this on dozens of occasions, using a big tin plate to keep the coals from scorching the earth and then dumping them back into the box afterward. Barrel fireplaces, if they are big enough, are a little better. You can push the fire to one side and balance your grill over the coals on a couple rocks or wood chunks. Some barrel fireplaces have a heavy hinged grate that can be lowered over the coals for cooking. The grate's iron bars may be spaced too far apart to keep hot dogs or steaks from slipping through the cracks; if so, cover the bars with your own grill.

Grill meats about 6 to 8 inches above softwood coals such as pine. Raise the grill a few inches higher if you have a hardwood fire. The hard woods, including oak, maple and apple, not only burn hotter than soft woods, but cleaner, as well. When you're stuck with poor wood, as you will be if you travel west to Rocky Mountain camping meccas such as Yellowstone Park, then consider adding a shovel-full of charcoal briquettes to supplement the natural coals.

Shish kebabs are an elegant, festive meal to cook on campfire coals.

Campfire Shish Kebabs
(SERVES FOUR TO SIX)

- 1 pound lean steak or cooked canned ham
- 1 large tomato
- 1 sweet onion
- 1 green pepper
- 1 can pineapple chunks
- 8 mushrooms
- Linda's Homemade Teriyaki Marinade (see next page)

Campfire Shish Kebabs with Linda's Homemade Teriyaki Marinade
(MAKES ENOUGH TO MARINATE A COUPLE OF POUNDS VENISON OR BEEF)

- 1 cup soy sauce
- ½ cup vegetable oil
- 3 tablespoons brown sugar
- 2 tablespoons white wine or cooking sherry
- 1 tablespoon powdered ginger
- 4 cloves minced garlic
- For jerky, add ¼ cup Worcestershire, 1 teaspoon Liquid Smoke and ¾ teaspoon pepper (for barbecue marinade, omit these ingredients)

Soak wooden skewers (buy the thickest ones you can find) in a pan of water while cutting up the veggies. Thread meat and vegetables onto skewers, spaced with the food pieces just kissing each other. Baste with marinade each time the skewers are turned. Because meat and vegetables can cook at different rates, you may want to separate them on different skewers.

Accompany your shish kebabs with corn on the cob in season. To cook corn on the grill, cut off the stem and slice through the husk at the small end. Don't peel the husk. Soak in water for a few minutes before grilling. (**Note:** Don't use river or lake water. It exposes you to the *Giardia* cyst, which is distributed by animal wastes and causes gastrointestinal illness, to put it politely). Turn cobs frequently over the fire. It's okay if the husks blacken a little. Just peel them back occasionally to make sure the corn isn't charring underneath.

As with all campfire recipes, cooking times are elastic. The corn is done when it's done. The key is not to be distracted. If you turn your back or let your attention stray, the flames will pick that moment to shoot up and ignite your meal.

Campfire shish kebabs are an easy and effective way to cook over a campfire. Although they take some preparation, once the skewers are ready, cooking them is a snap.

Grilled Venison or Beef Steaks
(SERVES FOUR)

- 4 steak medallions cut from elk, moose, beef, or deer backstraps, each about 1 inch thick
- 2 slices bacon, sliced in half lengthwise to make 4 narrow slices
- 2 garlic cloves (minced)
- A little thyme
- 1 tablespoon olive oil
- Cracked peppercorns

Rub steaks with olive oil, thyme, and minced garlic. Pepper to taste, keeping in mind that children will balk at too much spice. Wrap a slice of bacon around the edges of each medallion, pinning in place with toothpicks (if you've forgotten toothpicks, whittle a few from a piece of firewood).

Place on the grill and watch with all the protective intensity of a tigress watching her cubs. Turn once, after about 5 minutes. To test for doneness, insert the tip of your knife about a third of the way into the steak. It should juice pink without looking raw. You can also use the touch method to test doneness. Press the tip of a forefinger against the flesh over your chin. If the streak feels this soft, it's rare. Press your forefinger against the cartilage on the tip of your nose, which is a little firmer. When the steaks offer the same resistance, they are medium. Get them off the grill pronto and serve with a packaged Béarnaise sauce (Swiss-Knorr makes one my children would just as soon eat even without a steak).

You can also try this decadent whiskey-cream sauce from Angus Cameron's *L.L. Bean Game & Fish Cookbook*.

Steak and a Dram Sauce

- 4 tablespoons butter
- 3 tablespoons cream
- 2 tablespoons Scotch whiskey
- ½ teaspoon thyme
- Grated cheese (Stilton, blue cheese, or a crumbly hard cheddar)
- Minced parsley, if you have any in camp

Melt butter in pan or skillet and add the cream, Scotch whiskey, and thyme. Crumble cheese on top of the steaks and drizzle with the sauce. Do your arteries a favor and try to forget how good this tastes until at least next summer.

Cooking in Foil

Potatoes baked in campfire coals are the perfect accompaniment to grilled meats. If you've parboiled your potatoes at home, just double-wrap them in foil and bury them in coals for 20 minutes or so. Raw potatoes, of course, will take longer. Get started an hour before dinner and use small to mid-size bakers. Don't try to hurry cooking by tossing them into the hottest part of the fire; the outside will turn to charcoal while the inside remains hard. Instead, scrape coals a little to the edge of the flames and heap a couple of inches of coals on top of the foil-wrapped potatoes. Replenish coals as needed. The potatoes are done when a fork pushes easily through the center.

Almost any food can be cooked in foil, including vegetables, hamburger, and cubed potatoes, even all three at once. To get a tight seal that won't leak, use the campfire foil wrap (see below). It's wise to double-wrap with regular foil, but a single thickness of heavy-duty foil should be enough.

Campfire Foil Wrap

- Tear a sheet of foil a little more than twice as wide as the width of the food to be wrapped.
- Place food in the middle of the shiny side of the sheet, add seasoning, a dollop of butter or margarine, and a little water if food lacks moisture of its own.
- Turn up the sides of the foil, bring the edges together, and turn down in small folds until you can't fold it any farther.
- Flatten the ends of the foil and roll the open edges to the center.

Foil-wrapped food can be cooked by laying it directly on the coals, covering with a few coals if it needs top heat, or by placing on top of the grill. This is also an easy way to reheat leftovers or keep side dishes warm while you are busy cooking.

You can fashion a makeshift skillet by wrapping several layers of foil around the forks of a stout stick. I once camped with my father in the Missouri River Breaks in northern Montana, which is to say nowhere. We had remembered the food but forgotten to pack the cook box. I had a roll of aluminum foil (it's as indispensable on a camping trip as duct tape and should be packed with emergency supplies). For four days we did all our cooking in or on foil, eating with utensils carved out of driftwood. I don't remember either of us losing weight.

Fish Cookery

To camp is to make a home by water. To make a home by water and not to fish is like moving to a ski town and never taking off your dress shoes. Even if you can resist the temptation, given

A beautiful rainbow trout caught in a western stream. Cooking fresh-caught trout over a campfire is one of the genuine pleasures of camping.

the opportunity, your children won't. They will walk up the bank with a bluegill twisting from the hook and offer it to you the way a cat drops a mouse at your feet. If you have never made meat from a living animal before, don't despair. Just insert the point of a knife in the fish's vent, run it up the belly, and scoop out the innards. Remove the gills and the fish is ready for the pan.

Small trout, particularly the delectable brook trout that inhabit many northern creeks and ponds, have such smooth, minuscule scales that their skins feel like an eel's. There is no need to scale them before cooking. Warm-water species, including perch, bluegills, and bass, have rough scales. Hold the fish down firmly against a board and scale it by scraping a knife blade against the grain of the scales. Another option is to skin the fish before cooking. Small fish, including most trout, can be cooked whole; larger ones such as bass or pike should be filleted. (If you are far enough down the river as an angler that you are catching big fish, then you probably don't need to read any further.)

A pan of fried brook trout must surely rank as one of the finest meals on earth. Browns, rainbows, and cutthroats aren't far behind. Simply set the skillet to sizzling with a little butter, margarine, oil, or bacon grease (Leon L. Bean, the founder of L.L. Bean, preferred his fish fried in pork fat) and add the fish—heads, tails, and all. Squeeze a little lemon juice on top if you have it, but nothing is really required beyond a sprinkling of salt and pepper. To prevent tiny trout from curling in the pan, make a couple of slashes with a knife blade down their sides. Turn the fish once or twice as the skin begins to crisp. When you suspect the fish are about ready, insert the point of a knife along the trout's lateral line, which runs down the middle of either side, and lift the flesh. It should peel easily away from the spine and verge on flaking. Remember to keep track of fish the kids catch. It often means something to them to eat their own trout.

Grilling adds a wonderful smoky aroma that complements the natural sweetness of most fish. Don't skin fish that you intend to grill over the fire. The skin will protect the flesh from searing. In fact, the fish may skin itself when you attempt to turn it over. Leave the skin sticking to the grill and simply scrape it into the fire after the meal.

This recipe for fish in foil is from my friend Bill "Mo" Morris, who inherited it from his grandfather, who fished Pennsylvania's trout streams at the turn of the century.

Mo's Grandfather's Trout
(PER SERVING)

- 1 medium-sized trout, about 14 inches
- Several slices of onion (optional)
- 1strip bacon (optional)
- 1 tablespoon butter
- Salt and pepper
- 1 teaspoon lemon juice or wedge of lemon
- 1 sheet heavy-duty foil

Rub shiny side of foil with butter. Salt and pepper the trout's body cavity and place it on the foil. Cover with onions and strip of bacon. Add lemon juice or place lemon wedge in body cavity. Fold foil as directed for campfire wrap and place the wrap over a bed of coals. Cover top of foil with coals. Bake about 15 minutes. This method works well with any fish.

None of these ways to prepare fish call for herbs, spices, or exotic oils. You can use a little tamari, rice vinegar, and ginger, for example, to impart an Asian flavor, but if the fish is good, no seasoning is necessary.

MAKING COFFEE

Coffee tastes better on a cold morning with a mist blanketing the shoreline and the mournful voice of a loon breaking its heart on the lake than it does anywhere on earth. As long as you use enough coffee, almost any way you brew it will make a cup to remember.

Today, the trickle-down effect of America's coffee craze has sent tentacles all the way to the sporting goods store. You can buy miniature plastic drip cones that use disposable paper filters to drip a single perfect cup of coffee. Then, after a first cup of high-octane java to open the eyes, you have the choice of switching to decaf for a second cup.

Plastic French presses are also available; you can succumb to temptation farther yet and buy a Mini Expresso Maker that is no bigger than your child's fist.

But there is something about coffee brewed in a traditional blue-enamel coffee pot that is best of all. If you are new to camping, nothing will make you look or feel like an old hand quicker than being the first in the morning to have a fire crackling and pot of camp coffee steeping on a flat stone beside the fire.

Camp Coffee

- Cold water
- Medium-coarse ground coffee (about 1 ½ tablespoon per cup of water for strong coffee)
- 1 eggshell (it's traditional, whether it helps to settle the grounds or not)
- A few tablespoons of dried chicory root (optional)

Add coffee and chicory to a pot of *cold* water. Drop in eggshell. Bring pot to a boil and immediately remove it from the fire (don't boil the coffee). Let it steep for 5 minutes, then add a couple of tablespoons of cold water to help settle the grounds.

For those who take cream in their coffee, try adding a little canned condensed milk instead. The sweet, creamy syrup mixes with the scent of the pines and the clean, cold air to offset the bitter goodness of the mud in some inexplicable but perfectly harmonious way. Condensed milk also keeps longer and is easier to pack than a carton of cream.

DESSERTS

If you're a Dutch oven cook, nearly any recipe for cake or cobbler can be adapted and risen with the coaxing of a few white-hot coals. Just remember to pre-mix and pack the ingredients at home. We also like to freeze extra chocolate chip cookie dough at home. (Actually, there's no such thing as extra cookie dough; the camp cook has to think down the road and hide a freezer bag of it in the very back of the freezer.) Keep the dough in the camp cooler (it stays good for about four days), and dole out enough each evening to bake everyone a couple of cookies around the campfire. Just remember to line the bottom of the Dutch oven with foil to keep the cookies from sticking.

By the time dinner's done, it's often growing dark and the cook won't feel like dirtying his oven or burning her eyes any longer in the smoke of a fire. One solution is to let the children cook their own personal pies with pie irons (see Cooking with Children, p. 62). Another solution, simpler yet, is to break open a box of store-bought cookies. Because camping is a celebration, consider splurging for deluxe cookies instead of the those that the kids are used to seeing in their school lunch bags.

Popcorn is an obvious choice. The tins are easy to pack, and shaking the popcorn over the burner is something even the very young can try their hand at. Just take the precaution of having children wear gloves when working near a flame. Watermelon is messy, takes up too much space in the cooler, and leaves its calling card for bears and other camp pests, but it seems to be a ubiquitous part of the camping experience nonetheless.

Of course, no trip would be complete without S'mores.

S'mores
(PER SERVING)

- 4 sections of graham cracker snapped into 2 matching pieces
- 1 section of Hershey's milk chocolate bar (the size of one cracker)
- 1 large marshmallow

Toast each marshmallow over the fire until it is browned and gooey. With the marshmallow still on the stick, place it over a graham cracker, add the chocolate square and smash into a sandwich with the other cracker. Withdraw the toasting stick from the marshmallow and eat this delicious, very messy camp creation. Keep wet napkins handy to wash faces.

Hot chocolate may not be considered dessert in civilized society, but in camp it qualifies. There's nothing better, really, than settling down before the fire, tired to the bone, and sipping a hot chocolate before retiring to the tent. The kids love it, especially if they can drop a few petite marshmallows on top and watch them swirl around like a galaxy of melting stars until they disappear.

COOKBOX

When my brother Kevin and I were children, my father built a pine cookbox with shelves and hinged doors. I believe he copied it from a blueprint for a sportsman's project in *Field&Stream*. It looked very authentic set up in camp, but it was a heavy, cumbersome contraption. Ground squirrels gnawed their way inside on its inaugural trip. After a couple of summers, we went back to packing the cookware in a cardboard box.

Four decades later, I'm still packing the cookware for our family in a box, having resisted the temptation to buy a fold-up camp kitchen (although the one pictured in the L.L. Bean camping catalog looks tempting). For a time, I used an old wooden Coca-Cola box. Somebody told me it was

The easiest and most convenient way to carry and store your camp cooking utensils is to purchase a kit that is self-contained.

worth money as an antique, but by then I'd already decided to retire it because it was too heavy. A few years later I came across one of those perforated, blue plastic crates grocers use to haul around milk cartons. It was the right size and had cut-outs that made convenient handles. It makes a sturdy shell for the cardboard cooking box and seems about perfect.

The fact is, if you can't pack all that you need in a single, fair-sized box, then you have too much cooking gear. In many campgrounds, it's strictly against regulations to leave cooking gear outside when you're not using it because of the bears, so it's nice to have a box that's light enough to carry around a few times a day without throwing your back out.

Cookbox Contents for a Week's Trip

- 12-inch steel skillet (long-handled skillets are more suitable for cooking over a fire than regular skillets)
- 10-inch nonstick skillet (ideal for pancakes)
- 3-quart steel or aluminum pot with lid
- 1-quart steel or aluminum pot with lid
- Plastic cups for each camper (each gets a different color)
- Mugs for adults' coffee and children's hot chocolate (insulated plastic mugs with lids are good in case the cup gets knocked over; they also keep drinks hot longer on chilly mornings)
- Coffee pot (blue-enamel, steel, or aluminum)
- Knife, fork, and spoon for every camper
- Flat Tupperware container for cooking utensils
- Steel spatula (for steel skillet)
- Plastic spatula (for nonstick skillet)
- Basting brush
- Metal plate to use in food preparation, as cutting board with heavy paper plate inside, and as makeshift holder for hot coals
- Kitchen knife*
- Corkscrew and can opener (if you have a Swiss Army knife *and* strong hands, separate tools are unnecessary)
- 1 roll heavy-duty foil
- Heavy-duty paper plates
- Plastic or aluminum cereal bowls

---

*The folding Opinel knife with wooden handle and lock-back design is the camp knife nonpareil. Get the model with the 5-inch blade for the cook box and the smaller #8 model for your pocket. Neither should set you back more than $12.

- 2 rolls paper towels (one can be stored in food box)
- Biodegradable dishwashing soap (optional)
- Kitchen scrub sponge
- 6 plastic grocery bags for sheathing pots and skillets that are blackened by fire
- 6 tall kitchen garbage bags
- Pot holder
- Small dish towel
- Apron (a good idea if working over a fire; also helps keep food odors off clothing in bear country)
- Small wooden cutting board (optional)
- Box of wooden matches

Nest skillets together and place some of the cups inside the coffee pot. Instead of packing salt and pepper shakers[†], tea bags, and small jars of cooking oil and sugar where they may become scattered and difficult to find, store them inside the 3-quart pot.

Additional Cooking Equipment (Pack elsewhere)

- 2 pie-irons (pack flat on the floorboards of van or car)
- 10-inch cast-iron Dutch oven (optional, stored underneath car seat until needed)
- Charcoal and lighter fluid
- Fold-down Army shovel for shoveling coals, digging cooking pits, etc.
- Work gloves for holding pots, tending campfire, hauling firewood
- Heavyweight plastic or vinyl tablecloth (pin it to the picnic table with stones on windy days)

If your family is planning to camp in primitive sites that don't have picnic tables, it's a good idea to buy a folding camp table (see Chapter 3). An upside-down canoe, raised a couple feet off the ground on logs or blocks, makes a good table surface as well.

DUTCH OVEN COOKING

Despite its name, the Dutch oven is an American invention credited to the eighteenth-century Pennsylvania Dutch, whose traveling salesmen sold their cookware to wagon trains on the hard road west. The Dutch oven's enduring popularity is testament to the versatility of

---

[†]The best camp salt and pepper shakers I've used have spring-loaded, plastic lids with rubber seals to keep out moisture. They are used by restaurants in southern coastal towns and can be mail-ordered through The Restaurant Store in Key West, Florida, phone (305) 294–7994.

The Dutch oven has inspired many cookbooks, but almost any kitchen recipe can be adapted. Many Dutch oven chefs prefer charcoal briquettes to campfire coals, because they regulate heat more precisely.

its design: a heavy, cast-iron pot with three legs and a flanged lid that is recessed to hold coals. Hung by its handle over the fire, the Dutch oven is a pot for stewing. Set on top of coals with more coals heaped on top, it becomes an oven. Take off the lid, turn it upside down on the coals, and presto—you have a griddle for frying steaks or eggs.

The Dutch oven has inspired many cookbooks, but almost any kitchen recipe can be adapted. Preheat the oven by setting both the pot and the lid on the coals (turn the lid upside down to keep ashes from the inside). To bake, place dough in the bottom of the oven, cover the pot, and heap coals on top of the lid with your camp shovel. Because the oven is usually set on coals near the fire, the side closest to the flames will get more heat. Turn it occasionally to compensate.

Many Dutch oven chefs prefer charcoal briquettes to campfire coals, because they can regulate heat more precisely. For a moderate baking temperature, use the rule of three. Take the diameter of the pot and subtract three for the number of coals to place underneath the legs. Add three to the diameter for the number to set on top of the lid. For example, if you are using a 10-inch oven (a practical size for a family of three to six people), cook with seven coals underneath and 13 resting on top of the lid.

This has never seemed like enough heat to me, probably because we camp among pine trees that make a very poor fuel. I always end up covering the lid with several inches of campfire coals to bake a batch of biscuits. Whatever type of fuel you use, try to keep about two-thirds of the heat on top of the lid.

Dutch Oven Stew
(SERVES THREE TO SIX)

- 2 pounds beef, venison, or chicken breast, cut into cubes
- 2 tablespoons olive oil or vegetable oil
- 2 large onions, quartered
- 8 carrots, sliced
- 4 or 5 potatoes, white or red
- 3 cups beef broth (use bullion cubes)
- 2 cloves garlic, minced or 1 teaspooon garlic powder
- Salt and pepper to taste
- 1 teaspoon each rosemary and thyme
- 2 teaspoons brown sugar
- 2 teaspoons lemon juice

Brown meat cubes in oil. Remove to plate and add onions and carrots to the bottom of the Dutch oven. Cook for three or four minutes and return the meat to the oven. Pour in the beef broth; add herbs, garlic, salt, and pepper. Add ½ cup red wine if you brought any to drink with dinner. Cover with the lid and set on coals. Keep the ingredients simmering by periodically adding new coals shoveled out of the fire. For stewing, unlike baking, you want about two-thirds of the heat underneath the oven for stewing. Cook for at least an hour, preferably more. Add potatoes about 45 minutes before dinner. When you take the oven off the coals, stir in the brown sugar and lemon juice.

You can cook this stew or any other in a pit dug at the side of the fireplace, which eliminates the need to keep the flames licking during long cooking times. (Digging a hole beside the fire ring won't be permitted in many organized campgrounds, so check regulations before you start in with the shovel.) Take your Army shovel and dig a hole about two feet square and almost as deep. Brown the meat, add the rest of the ingredients and the liquid, then shovel coals from your breakfast fire into the bottom of the pit. Set the Dutch oven in the pit and heap more coals around the sides and on top of it. If it looks like you're running a little low, add a few charcoal briquettes to the mix.

Cover with dirt and go about your day. When you return, dig up the Dutch oven and brush the dirt off. Dinner's ready.

(**Note:** I wouldn't recommend pit cooking in bear country. A grizzly that burns a foot digging up your dinner is not likely to feel very agreeable when you arrive back in camp!)

Dutch Oven Buttermilk Biscuits

- 2 cups all-purpose flour (not self-rising)
- 2 teaspoons baking powder
- ¼ teaspoon baking soda
- 1 teaspoon salt
- ¼ cup butter or stick margarine
- ¾ cup buttermilk

Pre-mix dry ingredients at home and place in self-locking plastic bag with recipe. At camp, dump mix into a large paper plate or bowl, cut in butter with two knives until chunks are smaller than peas. Stir in buttermilk with a spoon.

Round up dough on paper plate and knead briefly. Roll to ½-inch thickness with a wine bottle or soda can. Cut out rounds with the mouth of a plastic cup and place them in the pre-heated oven bottom. They should not quite touch each other. Bake about 10 minutes, but peek in once or twice to check progress.

When biscuits are done, turn lid upside down and scramble eggs on the concave inside surface. Serve biscuits with blueberry or huckleberry jam. The kids will love it.

You also can bake coffee cakes, bread, pies, or cakes in a Dutch oven. Box mixes work well. Just line the bottom of the oven with foil or use a pie tin to keep the bottom of pies or breads from burning.

A good cast-iron Dutch oven[†] will cost between $20 and $60, depending on size. The companies that sell them also offer accessories, including pot covers, shovels, handle lifters, and cookbooks. They're nice but not necessary. A camp shovel and a properly whittled stick to lift the lid is all you need. However, it is necessary to season the oven before its first use, so pay attention to the instructions.

[†]Two sources for Dutch ovens are Kamper's Kettle, 2165 Bruneau, Boise, ID 83709, phone (208) 377–0344, and Lodge Manufacturing Co., P.O. Box 380, South Pittsburg, TN 37380, phone (615) 837–7181.

CHAPTER 6

The Catalyst of Fire

"Fire is the most tolerable third party."
HENRY DAVID THOREAU

More than any other facet of camping life, fire is the catalyst that bonds the fragmented lives of modern families. It is the magic candle of wilderness, a hearth away from home.

Generational differences melt before fire. Children who answer questions about school with a yes or no at home elaborate when they sit before flames. They tell stories of who likes whom, or who did what to whom, making you realize that the first gossip was probably traded between mouthfuls of mammoth before a roaring blaze. The kids sing songs their teachers never hear, with the worms crawling in, the worms crawling out, the worms playing pinochle in your snout, and adults who have not stretched their vocal cords in decades join the chorus.

Fire is a natural forum for story telling, as well. Ghost stories, no doubt, were invented by someone sitting in front of a fire. They rise like spirits from the flames, while golden light casts shadows across spellbound faces. Like a hypnotist's watch, fire's metronome of flickering light transports you to a world of dreams and memories. Sooner or later, all who sit before a fire fall victim to its trance.

My father was a magician with a campfire. He would bring a twist of newspaper to his cigarette, lighting it with a quick pull that made his cheeks hollow before lowering it to the kindling. Other times he would astound us by seeming to pull a lighted wood match out of his trousers pocket.

When the gnarled oak limbs my brother and I dragged from the Michigan woods started to snap, Dad would bring his pipe from his pocket, unzip his pouch of tobacco, and light up with a glowing twig. Mom would settle herself in a lawn chair with the cat in her lap.

A campfire can be the catalyst that brings together the fragmented lives of modern families. It is the magic candle of wilderness, a hearth away from home.

Every night, the four of us had that hour around the fire as a family. Kevin and I would roast marshmallows. Mom would shuffle her chair as the smoke sought her, while Dad spoke in the low, relaxed tones that sometimes eluded him in urban life. At dusk, he would pump up the lantern and string his fly rod. Down on the river, the mayflies were forming black ropes in the sky in preparation to dropping their eggs onto the water. In another hour they would float spent-wind down the current, drifting like crucifixes to the waiting trout.

My brother and I were too young to accompany him in those early years. But we joined in his ritual by spraying a pungent halo of bug spray around the brim of his hat and followed him as far as the riverbank, watching while his silhouette parted the moonlight on the water. Then we'd turn back to see the glint of light where our mother warmed her legs before the fire.

Nights such as these are among the most cherished memories of my childhood. That is why it's so disheartening to me to witness the lights dying out of today's campgrounds. I've taken my children on walks through the Madison Campground in Yellowstone National Park, which has more than 200 sites, knowing that when we returned, our tent would be easy to find because it was one of the few that shone with a beacon of fire.

Some of the campers we pass on our walk would have been out too late sightseeing to be bothered collecting wood. Perhaps others didn't want to smell smoke on their clothes in the morning. A few may even have turned their backs on fire because they consider burning wood to be ecologically unsound. That's an admirable stance in fragile alpine environments or arid areas, where fuel is scarce. But in many places, a century of fire-fighting policy has resulted in forests becoming littered with deadfall. This surplus of fuel creates the potential for

Singing songs around a campfire is a tradition that is rare in modern America, but when the opportunity arises, it is still great fun.

devastating infernos, and in popular camping destinations like Yellowstone (which suffered the consequences of its fire-fighting policy in the great fires of 1988), collecting downed timber for campfires is permitted and encouraged.

My own suspicion is that many younger people forgo fire simply because it has never had a place in their lives. They live in homes where the fireplace is only a decoration, where artificial flames are made with push of a button rather than the striking of a match. They retire to their tents warm, but not *warmed*, hungering for an ancestral hearth they have never known.

COLLECTING WOOD

Collecting firewood is something to think about earlier rather than later in the day. Those who are truly farsighted might consider bringing a box of split wood from home, and a camper who packs his own wood in rainy weather is wise indeed. But just as work expands to fit the time allotted, camping gear expands to fit the cargo space of a car. There never seems to be space left over for a woodbox and, besides, parents who pack their wood rob children of one of camping's fundamental chores.

In camp, the sources of wood closest at hand are the campsites themselves. Sometimes, previous tenants will have left a supply. Scrounging firewood is a time-honored tradition and a good campground chore for children. Just remind them not to take anything from a site that

A Brief History of Fire

According to Greek mythology, Prometheus stole fire from the gods and gave it to man. According to anthropological theory, man skipped the intermediary and took it directly from the earth, from flames ignited by a lightning strike. Where or when this happened first, no one will ever know. The oldest hearthsite discovered to date is on the floor of a limestone cave in France. It is made of fire-cracked stones, set in a circle a meter in diameter, similar to the fire rings in many campgrounds today. It is three-quarters of a million years old.

The ancient man-creature who built it, *Homo erectus*, was stooped and heavily built, with a sloped forehead, bony protuberances on his brows, and a jutting jaw. His taming of fire would alter the course of human evolution in several ways. Fire's warmth would render the heavy pelt on his chest and back superfluous, and his descendants would shed hair. Firelight would extend his day, so that hours could be spent before its brilliant candle, crafting weapons, skinning game for clothing, planning hunts for tomorrow. No longer would his clan have to gather at the site of a kill to eat; instead, hunters would bring the meat into the cave, where the torch protected him from predators and cooked his kills.

Because spitted venison was easy to chew, the great muscles needed to tear and render raw meat were no longer exercised. Man's jaw and great brow, where these muscles attached to bones, began to recede, giving the skull more room for the developing brain. So fire came to change the contours of his face, the very capacity of his thought.

With the advent of the hearth, man had both the forum and the leisure to practice his new-found powers of speech. And it was his speech that set him down the path to civilization.

Before man developed the skill to strike his own spark, he had to depend on God's thunderbolts to provide it for him. Flame thus stolen from grass or forest fires was precious indeed, for a year might pass before it swept the country again, and the lives of the entire clan were dependent upon its constant tending through seasons of rain and snow. So the keepers of flame rose to great stature in the culture, and devised many ingenious ways to keep their fires alight.

Perhaps it was one of these fire tenders who discovered that striking iron pyrite with a piece of flint showered white-hot sparks, or that the friction of a stick rubbed vigorously upon a stump created smoke, from which could be made the greatest magic.

Is it any wonder that builders of fire were breeders of myth, or that fire became so worshipped by some in our ancestry that human sacrifices were made to its spirits?

This is the heritage we carry to our own campfires hundreds of thousands of years later. You can tell this history of fire to your children some night when the ghost stories have worn a little thin. It may give them an appreciation for the flames they take for granted.

has a rope across the parking space or a stub of paper indicating that it's reserved. After they come back, dragging their dribs and drabs of sticks along the ground, pull on the work gloves and fish the blackened wood out of the campfire rings that the kids disdained to touch. Charcoal makes an excellent bed to build your fire upon.

The wooded edge of the campground most likely will have been thoroughly scavenged by other campers. Even if it isn't, avoid collecting downed wood so close by. Swiping every log mars the natural beauty of the forest and can upset the ecological balance. Far better to pile the family into the car, after disgorging it of camping gear, and drive a mile or more down the road. On most public lands, removing dead, downed timber is permitted; however, be careful to obey local regulations.

Don't take any standing wood and check to make sure that what you do collect is dry. If branches bend without snapping, they're too green. Green wood is difficult to ignite and tends to smolder, filling your site with smoke. Punky, rotted wood that is in the process of decomposing on the forest floor also burns poorly. Seasoned wood that snaps readily and has been exposed to the sun is best, so search the edges of open areas or light forest where the sunlight penetrates.

The place to haul wood is on the braces of a car-top carrier. Leave a couple of heavy-duty bungee cords permanently attached, to simplify securing the load.

How much wood do you need? An armful of dense hardwood sticks as big around as your wrist may be enough for a couple of evening campfires, with enough left over to cook breakfast the third morning. Hickory, beech, oak, and maple are among the best woods for fire in the East. In some parts of the Southwest, mesquite is very common. It makes a hot, long-lasting fire, not to mention the best bed of coals for cooking you could hope to find. But if you're camping in the pines, you'll need at least twice as much pine as you would of any hard wood. Pine burns with about half the BTU value of oak or hickory, and as quickly as it kindles, its candle goes out.

BUILDING THE CAMPFIRE

The quickest way to start a fire is to make a collection of small sticks, run a thin stream of charcoal lighter over them and toss a match. This method is safe enough if you don't use much lighter fluid. You should never start fire with gasoline or any other explosive liquid. No doubt more campfires are started with newspaper than anything else. But if sharpening wilderness skills and passing them along to the next generation is important to you, practice fire-making with natural tinder and a single match.

Get children involved in the process by sending them on a treasure hunt for tinder while you are busy hunting for larger wood. Pine needles that have dried out and turned orange are an excellent fire starter, whereas dry leaves are relatively poor. The petals of old pine cones, abandoned bird nests, dry moss, lichen, and dried grasses all start fires readily. If you're lucky enough to be camping in an eastern river bottom, peel and shred the inner bark of a downed birch log; it is probably nature's best tinder, burning with a strong flame even when wet. A child who is old enough to be trusted with a knife can be taught to make a *fuzz-stick* by peeling curl after curl from a stick, detaching as few curls as possible so that the end of the stick comes to look like a sheaf of wheat. Emergency tinder includes paper money, fuzz in shirt and pants pockets, and the loose threads at the tops of socks. The rewards of teaching children how to find tinder go beyond an education in starting fires; they include lessons in natural history and making do with what's at hand.

The quickest way to start a fire is to make a teepee of small sticks, run a thin stream of charcoal lighter over it, and toss a match. You can also build your teepee of sticks over dry paper or birch bark, then light the tinder.

Next, round up a collection of small sticks. The dead, resinous twigs that quill the lower trunks of evergreens are one of nature's best sources of matchstick-size wood. Protected from rain and snow by a thick canopy of needles, these twigs are nearly always dry and have probably saved the lives of more people lost in the woods than the compass.

Keep sending the kids back for sticks until they have made three piles, one of match-sized sticks, a second of pencil-sized sticks, and a third of sticks the diameter of a finger. A double handful of the match-sized sticks will suffice, but have them add to the piles of larger sticks until they are each the size of a loaf of bread. That ought to be enough to start several fires.

Back in camp, have one child roll the tinder into a loose mass about the size of a billiard ball. Then build a tepee of kindling over it, starting with the matchsticks and progressively increasing the size of the wood as the teepee grows taller. The children can help. The wood teepee should be about a foot tall and a foot in diameter, rather loosely constructed to permit air circulation.

To light the fire, insert a wood match through a gap on the windward side of the teepee, just under the tinder. You may find that blowing very softly on the tinder will help it catch flame. And keep the piles of sticks handy, should it look like you need to add more kindling.

Don't be discouraged if your first efforts fail. Building a fire with natural tinder takes practice and patience and can be difficult even for adults.

Paraffin blocks and other commercially made fire starters are available in sporting goods stores. They simplify fire starting with damp wood and should be part of the kit of every hiker and backpacker.

TYPES OF FIRES

Unless the night is very cold or a big bed of coals is needed for the Dutch oven, keep your campfire small. Small fires are not only

---

A Kid's Project

Making your own fire starter is a great children's project. Here are three home recipes they can try out in camp:

- Drop paraffin or candle stumps in a tin can and set in a pot of simmering water. When the wax is melted, remove the can and drizzle the wax over cotton balls. Or simply carry cotton balls to the campground and smear them with petroleum jelly. Insert them underneath the tinder and light.

- Make a 3-inch diameter newspaper log by rolling several newspapers tightly and binding them with masking tape. Then cut the log into two-inch sections with a fine-toothed saw. Kids can roll smaller-diameter logs with newspapers cut into 4-inch strips. Soak the log sections in melted paraffin, let them dry, and seal them in plastic bags. Insert one under the kindling.

- Fill each cup of an egg carton with shredded newspaper and drizzle melted paraffin over the top. Tear off a single cup each time you need to start the fire.

---

safer, but teach children lessons about waste and economy, allow you to sit closer to each other, and have a charm unmatched by larger blazes.

To maintain a small hardwood fire, simply add a few pieces of broken branch, an inch or two in diameter, to the teepee as it burns and collapses in on itself. Criss-cross branch sections over each other to maintain air circulation, being careful not to burn your fingers. Work gloves help protect against errant flames. When the fire starts to die down, take your poking stick and turn over the burnt wood. That will cause it to flare up again, and you can put off adding more fuel a little longer. Once you have a good bed of coals, a couple of small log pieces, laid parallel to each other, will keep a flame going in the valley between them for a long time.

The traditional large, communal campfire is the log-cabin fire, which is just what it sounds like—a Lincoln log home of crossed logs built over top of an unlit tepee fire with a log roof over top. The drawback to the log-cabin fire is that it burns the fuel supply all at once. Better to continually feed a teepee fire more and larger pieces of wood until a blaze is roaring, then stack a couple of larger log sections at the back for a firebreak.

Always be careful to match the size and shape of the fire to the fire ring provided at the campsite. Beware that soft woods such as pine can spit embers a long distance.

CAMPFIRE CUTLERY: SAWS, AXES, AND BONES TO GRIND

The saw and the ax have become all but obsolete in today's campgrounds. Little wonder, then, that the number of campers who build fires is diminishing, for without these tools, maintaining flame with pine or damp woods can be difficult. Pine branches scoured from the forest floor often are either too green or pulpy and decomposed to burn. Along with roots and knots, which are resinous, the best pine for fires comes from larger sections of dry tree trunks. With relatively little surface area for oxygen circulation, these trunks burn poorly in the round. Sawing them into foot-long chunks and then splitting with an ax exposes more wood surface to the air, and the more splintered the splits are, the better they will burn. They same is true for wet wood.

Your local sporting goods store will have several models of saw to choose from. You also can order a good wood-cutting saw from the L.L. Bean catalog. The best saw for serious firewood rendering is the Swede or bow saw, with a gaptoothed cross-cut saw blade from 20 to 36 inches long and a D-shaped handle made of tubular steel. That sounds big, but a bow saw is much more efficient than a collapsible backpacking saw and can be packed flat, taking up little cargo space.

A three-quarter size or slightly smaller Hudson Bay ax is about right for splitting four- to six-inch diameter pine. Larger wood blocks are better split with a maul.

Hatchets are fine for cutting sticks, but they are too light for wood splitting.

A three-quarter size Hudson Bay ax is all you need to split smaller logs. Hatchets are good for cutting sticks, but are too light for serious wood splitting and can be dangerous in the hands of a child.

Being short-handled, a hatchet is more dangerous than an ax in the hands of a child; the head of an ax is farther away from tender extremities.

EXTINGUISHING THE CAMPFIRE

It's easy to poke fun at Smokey the Bear, who admonished campers to put their fires out—"dead out." After all, how dangerous can a few dying embers be?

The answer is: very dangerous. Coals will smolder for hours under hot stones or logs. In fact, coals from forest fires have been known to survive a blanket of winter snow and flare up again in the spring. All it takes is a little night breeze, a spark that falls a foot out of the campfire ring, a dry blade of grass.

Splitting Firewood

The safest way to split a section of log is to wedge it between two other logs, or to place it upright in the crotch of a downed log, in the angle where a heavy branch is attached to the trunk. Then raise the ax in a short arc and bring it back down squarely on the block. If the ax head sticks in the wood without splitting it all the way, lift the log section with the ax handle and drive it down again until it splits. Most campers split wood by setting a section of log upright on top of a stump or chopping block. That's okay if no one is around, but beware that this method causes the splits to fly apart and can injure someone standing nearby.

Teach your children that although it is all right to use a foot or a hand to steady a log they want to *saw*, they should never try it when using an ax. In fact, they shouldn't be using an ax until the age of 10 or so, depending upon their maturity. Saws can be used safely at younger ages with proper supervision.

Swing the head at arm's length from your body. Instruct kids to use short strokes, instead of bringing the ax head high overhead, and don't swing the ax where it could glance off a rock or other hard object. Never split firewood around other children playing in camp, who might careen out of control into the arc of the bit.

When dousing the campfire, always add that second bucket of water and kick over the logs to drown the coals underneath. Then stir the ashes with your poker and add a little more water.

Campfires are our heritage, but building them is not an inalienable right. If our children's children are to experience sitting before them, we must not abuse the privileges we now enjoy.

CHAPTER
7

Into the Night

"Now I see the secret of the making of the best persons,
It is to grow in the open air,
and to eat and sleep with the earth."

WALT WHITMAN

In wilderness, the light of evening seems not to fade so much as to draw farther away. For a while it burns on mountain tops, like the wicks of candles before they go black. Closer to camp, trees begin to blur. The creek that seemed silent by day speaks in a faint but insistent murmur. And a human being who felt at home in the woods an hour earlier steps out of the firelight and is suddenly a little smaller than he was before.

Most adults can temper a natural fear of the dark with reason. But to a child, night can be very scary. Children have vivid imaginations, and until they become comfortable sleeping outdoors, every leaf stirred by midnight's wind is a paw scratching at the tent flap. If they are to enjoy a good night's sleep, they must first be reassured of their safety.

Ghost stories that enthrall ten-year-olds may be inappropriate for younger brothers or sisters. Be considerate and try not to add to instinctive fears just before bedtime. Instruct older kids to wait until the young ones have gone into the tent before they retell the old chestnut of the couple who drove away from Lovers' Lane just in the nick of time, with the steel hook of the murderer hanging from their door handle. And on nights when you'd like to spend a little more time by the fire after your children have gone to bed, wait until they are asleep or you are certain their fears have been assuaged before sneaking back outside the tent.

The last light from the setting sun—a reflection of peace and harmony on a mountain lake. We seldom have time in our fast-paced daily lives to appreciate nature's beauty. Learn to slow down. Listen. Watch.

SLEEPING ARRANGEMENTS, SLEEPING AIDS

Very young children will feel more secure sleeping between adults than at the edge of the tent. They also will feel closer to parents if a large comforter or blanket covers everyone, rather than each person being cocooned in isolated sleeping bags. Of course, the temperature plays a large part in sleeping arrangements. But as a general rule, make sleeping in camp a communal experience. Individual tents or zippered sleeping compartments in large tents may sound tempting to couples, but realistically, they are options to look at only when the kids are older.

Flashlights are one of the cheapest investments you can make in a child's courage. Buy flashlights in different colors so that everybody has one to call his own. Because kids are careless and often forget to turn their flashlights off, running down the batteries, choose models that twist on and off instead of those that use a button. If someone does hear a noise in the night, don't say it's nothing and tell him or her to go back to sleep. Shine your light outside and reassure everyone that it was only the wind.

For years, I've made it a tradition to read a story when we are all together in the tent. Usually it is something with a light touch, like one of Kipling's classic "'Just So' Stories." I'm not sure whether it's because the sound of my voice is soothing or because it masks outside noises, but by the time I know how the camel got his hump, my children and my wife are usually asleep.

SAFETY CONCERNS

Probably the most common concern parents have is keeping their children warm enough on crisp nights. Although it is natural to err on the side of safety and pile comforters and blankets on top of sleeping bags, too much insulation is just as bad as too little. We took Tom and Jessie camping when they were less than a year old, in temperatures that fell into the teens at night, and never had the slightest problem. Children who are too cold will squirm and shiver; if they are lying next to you, you'll know when they need another cover.

Anyone who's done much camping has seen the silhouettes of neighbors who have brought their lanterns inside the tent. The golden glow looks inviting, and I'll be the first to admit that for years one of those silhouettes was me. I was careful, always setting the lantern several feet away from both the sleeping area and the tent walls, where it was unlikely to be accidentally kicked over. But during one of the summers I worked on a river crew in Michigan, I fell asleep reading and woke up in the middle of the night to find my lantern on its side, knocked over by the wind (it was a hot night and I had left my tent flap open). A piece of the globe, which had been cracked and was held together with metallic tape, had fallen onto the floor of the tent and underneath it the canvas had burned away in a big circle, exposing the grass. The lantern was down to the cherry glow of the mantles by the time I found it, but the canvas was still smoldering and even a brash kid like me could see that the story could have had a different ending.

Today's tent materials have to pass a flame retardancy test, but they are still flammable, as is much of the gear you will have scattered about. We recommend using a big, six-volt flashlight lantern inside a tent instead of using a gas or propane lantern.

Today's tent materials have to pass a flame retardancy test; even so they are flammable, as is much of the gear you will have scattered about. Taking a gasoline or propane lantern inside a tent is asking for trouble. (In a trailer with the windows closed, a lantern poses a different danger, as it eats up all the available oxygen.) It's much safer to carry a big, six-volt flashlight lantern for indoor use.

Always zip the tent securely at night. If someone small has to go to the bathroom, get your flashlight and accompany them. Children who are unescorted are not only more susceptible to falling and getting hurt, but they can become disoriented. I remember walking to the outhouse at night when I was a boy, then opening the door a minute later and not knowing which way to turn. Anxiety can quickly turn to panic, and by the time a child begins to cry for help he may be too far away for you to hear.

SLEEPING PADS: THE FOUNDATION OF A GOOD NIGHT'S SLEEP

Trailers and tent trailers are equipped with thick foam pads that make the transition from bed almost unnoticeable. But in a tent, lying on uneven ground, your chance of a good night's sleep is almost entirely dependent upon the padding underneath your body. In the old days of canvas wall tents with dirt floors, cots were the most practical foundation on which to build a camp bed. However, their popularity has waned in recent decades. Cots are heavy, although most fold down compactly enough, and many designs tend to sag in the middle. Space is another problem. Within the concave walls of smaller dome tents, there just isn't enough room for them. However, if you have the luxury of a big car and a big tent, a good-quality cot that offers even support and a thick foam mattress is hard to beat, especially in rainy weather, when the tent floor is likely to become damp. Also, the cot's elevated structure means there is floor space underneath to stow boots and gear.

Air mattresses also are out of vogue. Even the best ones leak sooner or later. Having no insulative value, they are worthless in cold weather unless you put a pad on top of them. Sleeping bags tend to slip off air mattresses, leaving you on the ground. With the larger air mattresses that sleep two or more, there is a ripple effect: the shifting weight of one person affects the others. I slept on a leaky air mattress for umpteen years, priding myself in perfecting the trick of falling asleep before it lost air. That conceit lost its appeal the older I grew. If you do opt for an air mattress, get a heavy, canvas and rubber one that can be inflated with a foot pump or an electrical pump; the kind that operates off a car battery is best. If the surface is slippery, try dribbling a few drops of Shoe Goo or Aqua Seal over the surface to make it sticky.

Thin, closed-cell pads come in a variety of designs—single layer, ridged, air-bob, or even accordion-style for easy folding. For a few dollars they offer remarkable insulative value, but most are not much more forgiving than the ground underneath them. Backpackers favor them because they can be rolled compactly and weigh next to nothing. But in camp, their usefulness is restricted to small children, who have the bones of birds and can practically sleep on rocks, and to serving as an insulative layer underneath thicker, more comfortable pads.

Open-cell foam pads like the ones with the popular eggshell pattern are cushy when new, but they offer little insulation and tend to collapse under heavy use. Plus, they take up a lot of space in the car. However, if you have room, they are superb for layering over closed-cell pads and contribute greatly to a good night's sleep.

The best compact pads for sleeping are the Therm-a-Rest and knockoff designs that incorporate an insulative foam pad inside an abrasion-resistant air mattress. They come in a variety of thickness and sizes. The three-quarter length is excellent for backpacking, but the full-size camp beds are more comfortable. They aren't cheap, but then neither is the value of sleep. You can compromise, as we have, by buying the pricier Therm-a-Rest (or knockoff-design) pads for the adults, while the kids make do with closed-cell pads, stacked two to a child for extra comfort.

SLEEPING BAGS, PILLOWS, AND OTHER CREATURE COMFORTS

Sleeping bags come in two basic designs: rectangular and mummy. Mummy bags, which are contoured to fit the body, are smaller and lighter in weight than rectangular bags. For a comparable amount of insulating material, they do a much better job of keeping heat from escaping and allow you to sleep more warmly. This feature is most desirable for backpackers, but can make a bag feel confining otherwise.

Mummy bags are contoured to fit the body—they are smaller and lighter in weight than rectangular bags and easier to stay warm in on cold nights.

The advantage of rectangular bags, besides the comfort of having foot room and being able to squirm around a little, is that on nights when it's not too cold, you can unzip the bag, lie down on a sheet and drape the bag over you as a comforter. Or if it's a hot night, spread the sleeping bag on top of the pads, lie down on top of it and cover up with the sheet. An unzipped sleeping bag also makes a perfect picnic blanket (except in areas where food odors might attract bears). Such versatility, of course, depends on the bag having a zipper that runs all the way down one side and across the bottom. Avoid models with a partial zipper.

The advantage of rectangular bags, besides the comfort of having more foot room and being able to squirm around a little, is that on nights when it's not too cold, you can unzip the bag and drape it over you like a comforter.

Goose down offers the greatest loft and warmth for its weight, but down is very expensive and loses all its insulating value when it becomes wet. For tent camping, polyester fill makes more sense. Cotton flannel liners are comfortable, but they can become uncomfortably damp in coastal areas or wet weather.

Double-size sleeping bags are fine for couples who sleep together like kittens on Christmas night. They also might be a good choice for a mother with a nursing baby. But other pairings, such as an adult with an older child, leave something to be desired. One person is hot, the other is cold, or someone gets kicked and can't fall back to sleep. Individual bags are usually better.

You can purchase infant and child-sized sleeping bags, even kid's bags with built-in extensions to accommodate growth. They're nice, but they aren't really necessary. An adult-sized bag is fine. Just keep in mind that a small body in a large bag won't stay as warm as a small body in a bag cut to fit it. To minimize heat loss from a large bag, fold the bottom half underneath the child's body. If more warmth is needed, add a blanket or comforter on top.

As far as pillows are concerned, the ones you use at home will be more comfortable and familiar than postage-stamp-sized camp pillows from the sporting goods store. Just keep a drawer-full of old pillowcases to draw from, so your best ones don't get dirty.

The same nightclothes children wear at home, whether they are pajamas or flannel nightgowns, are perfectly appropriate for most camping situations. It's much better they be comfortable in clothes they're used to than attempt to sleep in play clothes or outfits that are stiff and new. And don't forget special companions like teddy bears; any form of security blanket to get a girl or boy through the night is well worth the space it takes up in the car.

SLEEPING WOES

There are three sleeping pills that wild places offer that no doctor can prescribe for you. They are the sound of running water, the patter of rain, and the salt breeze off the ocean. The gentle shush of a nearby waterfall can lull anyone into peaceful slumber.

My son Tom once complained that he didn't like overnight birthday parties. He said he spent most of the night listening to other kids sleep. I told him that was a sign of intelligence, because that's what my mother told me when I made the same complaint thirty-five years ago.

Insomnia sufferers suffer the most away from home, and a cramped sleeping bag in a campground halfway across the country is about as far away from your bedroom as you can get. But there are a few tricks you can use to ease the transition.

Always lie with your head slightly elevated. Bring an extra blanket, an extra pillow to compensate for irregularities of the ground, and an extra pad, and don't let anyone shame you into sharing the wealth. Often the most comfortable way to sleep is with the bag partially zipped and a light blanket pulled over the top half of your body. If it's cold, wear a wool or fleece watch cap to avoid having to bury your head in the sleeping bag. In fact, you should have sleeping hats for every member of the family, though I've yet to meet a child who can keep one on all night.

If you sleep on the right side of the bed at home, roll out your bag accordingly in camp. If you're accustomed to reading at night, bring a small flashlight with extra batteries to facilitate the routine. Drape a handkerchief over the lens to dim the beam and avoid disturbing others. If you wake up having to use the bathroom, don't lie around for an hour working up the courage to clamber out of the tent. Have your shoes and your flashlight handy and do it. You might want to bring earplugs in case the noises of neighbors or the snores of your companions are distracting.

Once they have fallen asleep, children are not as bothered by noise as adults, nor do they wake up to use the bathroom as often. The key to a good night's sleep is to make them feel secure and see that they use they use the bathroom *before* they go to bed. On the chance that they do wake up, comfort them with an extra blanket if they feel cold, and talk in a soothing voice until they fall back to sleep.

There are three sleeping pills wild places offer that no doctor can prescribe for you, and all of them work equally well for children or adults. They are the sound of running water, the patter of rain, and the salt breeze off the ocean. I have visited two campgrounds in my life-time, one on Prince Edward Island and another along the Oregon coastline, that on some nights have offered all three. Upon such sorcery I have drifted to distant lands and returned as a new man. They are worth more to me, or to anyone who has trouble sleeping at night, than gold, frankincense, and myrrh.

SECTION
III

Exploring the Outdoors

CHAPTER 8

Wildlife and Recreation

> " . . . [T]he book of nature has no beginning, as it has no end. Open the book where you will, and at any period of your life, and if you have the desire to acquire knowledge you will find it of intense interest; and no matter how long or how intently you study the pages your interest will not flag, for in nature there is no finality."
>
> JIM CORBETT

I have a friend whose most treasured days of summer start early, when heavy mists carpet the lakes in Montana's Red Rocks Lakes National Wildlife Refuge. That's when Kim Kotur likes to paddle her canoe to see the trumpeter swans, bitterns, and black-crowned night herons for which the refuge is nationally famous. The only problem is getting her son to climb out of the tent, for at 48 degrees latitude, the sun rises very early.

One day, Kim was exasperated as she turned to the open door of the tent and for the third time cajoled little Mike, then four years old, to rise and shine.

"Come on, get up and see the crack o' dawn," Kim said.

"Crack-a-don!" he shouted excitedly, sitting bolt upright in his sleeping bag. "Where! Where!"

My friend said that this is a trick that only works at the age when children take plastic dinosaurs into their beds at night. Nonetheless, the result was that her son did get up to accompany her in the canoe and marvel at the great rafts of waterfowl. Today, thanks to his mother's efforts to teach him about nature, Mike can identify all the waterfowl and shorebirds in the state and will undoubtedly pass on the love of the outdoors to his own children.

Waking sleepy children can be challenging, but they have the best chance of seeing wildlife by hitting the trail at first light.

Kids who become excited about wildlife or any other facet of nature are simply those who have been exposed to it by their parents. Children have an inherent fascination for all wild things, but you need to do more than talk about them to sustain a lasting interest. You must

Some states, like Montana, have a "watchable wildlife" division that distributes maps and guidebooks of the best areas to see certain wildlife species.

lead by example, preferably when your children are young and most impressionable. If that means dragging them out of bed at an ungodly hour, then so be it.

Unfortunately, most campers are either sleeping or sitting around with an after-dinner coffee at the best times to observe birds and animals. Larger mammals are most active at dawn and dusk. If you want your children to see nature's biggest drawing cards, such as the grizzly bears and wolves of Yellowstone Park, you need to have your binoculars in hand not long after the stars have faded from the sky.

STRATEGIES FOR WATCHING WILDLIFE

The key for getting a family up and out to look for wildlife is to keep early morning preparations simple. Breakfast, except for a handful of trail mix, a granola bar, or a slice of banana bread, can wait until you return from wildlife viewing. You can also eat dinner early, in order to leave the last daylight hours free from chores.

In parks such as Yellowstone, the safest and most productive way to observe wildlife is from your car. In many other places the best way to see wildlife is by hiking or slowly walking along the wooded edges of misty meadows. Canoes offer a quiet, peaceful entry into the

Keeping Your Distance

Be aware that many animals resent a close approach and will react by fleeing or, on rare occasions, attacking the intruder. Kids have a natural inclination to get as close to animals as possible and you must explain to them why they shouldn't. Loons, for example, raise tremulous voices when boats come close. Many boaters, who assume the birds are simply calling to one another, don't realize they are alarming the loons, which resent intrusion at a much greater distance than other waterfowl.

Larger animals can be dangerous when approached too closely. The critical distance varies with the species and the circumstances, but generally speaking, stay at least 30 yards from elk or moose and double your respect, and distance, from bison and black bears. If you can see a grizzly bear clearly without binoculars, you're too close.

A few other rules of thumb for safe wildlife watching include:

- Don't come between rutting male elk or bison and herds of females.

- Beware of all females with young, not just bears. Moose and bison are extremely protective of their calves and have been known to charge intruders.

- An animal that pricks its ears up and stares at you is alarmed. Back off.

- Bighorn sheep and mountain goats often pay little attention to hikers below them. They resent intrusion from above.

- Never turn and run from an aggressive animal. Stand tall, keep the family close together, and back away slowly. See Chapter 9 for recommendations for hiking safely in bear country.

Binoculars

Binoculars not only permit a closer look at birds and animals, but can gather light that enables the viewer to see more clearly than is possible with the naked eye. They come in two basic styles, poro-prism and roof-prism, and in various powers, such as 7×35, 8×40, 10×50, and so on. The first number denotes the magnification. The second number refers to the size in millimeters of the objective lens, which determines how much light the glass can gather. Generally speaking, an 8×40 binocular will gather more light than an 8×32 binocular, and give you a lot clearer look at wildlife in periods of low light. The tradeoff: larger objective lenses translate into greater weight.

More than any other piece of camping gear I can think of, with binoculars you get what you pay for. The quality and coating on the lenses is much more important than either the style, the power, or the focusing mechanism. Cheap binoculars will cause eyestrain, gather little light, and blur the image you are looking at. Buy the best binoculars you can afford. For most wildlife viewing, 7×35 or 8×40 binoculars offer a good balance of power and light-gathering capability without being too heavy. Birdwatchers may opt for 9- or 10-power, but the higher the magnification, the more difficult it is to hold binoculars steady enough to keep the image from trembling. Tiny compact binoculars are convenient to carry, but their resolution and light-gathering capacity suffer. Avoid variable-power binoculars. A few are good, but most are marketing gimmicks and are cheaply made.

Before purchasing binoculars, check to see that the eyepieces can be adjusted to fit the small faces and close-set eyes of children. Kids often have trouble finding an animal in binoculars, which is another reason for opting for lower powers, which have wider fields of view.

Spotting scopes are similar to telescopes in shape and typically come in variables from about 15- to 40-power. These scopes are specialty items that you need not consider unless your family is planning a trip to Alaska or a national park, such as Glacier, that offers long-distance viewing opportunities of grizzly bears, wolves, bighorn sheep, and mountain goats. Tripods are necessary to steady spotting scopes for observation.

world of nature, and allow you to approach much closer to waterfowl and small aquatic mammals such as muskrats, otters, and beaver than you'd be able to otherwise. Moose and deer that are typically wary of human beings will often pay little attention to a canoeist gliding by.

In many national parks, naturalists lead guided tours through wildlife habitat. Check at the ranger station or campground booth for schedules. Other sources of information are state fish and wildlife agencies. For example, Montana has a "watchable wildlife" division that distributes maps and guidebooks of the best areas to see certain species. The state also erects signs painted with the image of binoculars to inform motorists of vantage points to observe wildlife and read about their habits.

THE WORLD AT YOUR FEET

Although birds of prey and larger animals are the marquee attractions of wilderness, children also should be encouraged to discover the secret lives of smaller animals. Spiders, snakes, frogs, lizards, and salamanders are as worthy of their attention as deer and eagles. They enable young people to bring the

Children should be encouraged to discover the secret lives of smaller animals like spiders, snakes, frogs, and toads. They enable young people to bring the miracle of nature directly to their fingertips.

miracle of nature directly to their fingertips and, unlike larger animals, they are usually easier to find.

I vividly remember the first snake I held in my hands, a garter snake my father found in the front yard of our home. The snake's handsome face and creamy stripes, its cool graceful body, captivated me so completely that for years the focus of my attention seldom raised any higher than the stones beside the path. Eventually, by turning one stone after another I uncovered a demure ring-neck snake in my mother's herb garden, which led in time to the powerful rat snake coiled under a ledge on the lip of a cliff. So the front yard led to the backyard and the woods beyond, to the tent beside the mountain stream and all those rooms of the forest I now call my home.

In some places, the presence of poisonous snakes or scorpions makes it unwise to lift stones or logs barehanded (see Chapter 9). A makeshift "snake stick" can be made from a 3- or 4- foot section of broom handle and a piece of angle iron (or steel) bought from a hardware store. Just use wire or duct tape to secure one wing of the angle iron to the base of the stick, so that the other juts out at a 90-degree angle. Use this lip to carefully lift flat stones (those with some visible space underneath them are more likely to house small creatures than ones stuck in the ground), clumps of grass, and pieces of bark. After examining your catch, gently release it and replace the disturbed stones or vegetation exactly as you found it.

Over the years, we have seen many children experience the discovery of nature's smallest inhabitants. A child's lifelong appreciation of wild things can start from this simple introduction.

Given an opportunity, most young children will become fascinated by the small inhabitants of our world. Like me, they may develop a lifelong appreciation and support for wild things from nothing more than a shadow or a whisper in the grass.

Many excellent guidebooks are available for the identification and study of insects, reptiles, and amphibians. By turning their pages, your children will discover the stardust at their feet as well in the lens of your binoculars.

ANIMAL TRACKS AND SCAT

Every bird and animal leaves traces of its passage by the impressions of its feet and droppings. Tracks are most easily read in snow, mud, sandy streambanks, dirt roads, and dusty game trails. Raccoons tracks will be found along many streambeds; by noting where the raccoons approach the water, you can often find the claws and shell fragments of crawfish they have eaten. You also can show kids the muddy trails through grass where beaver have dragged trees and sticks into the water.

Larger animals leave oval-shaped depressions of flattened vegetation or depressions in the snow where they have bedded down. These beds are often more easy to find than tracks, especially in areas where the ground is hard or the ground cover is dense.

If you are lucky enough to experience a light snowfall during a camping trip, it is sometimes possible to follow a set of deer or elk tracks and catch sight of the animal that made them. I have led several kids on such stalks, which stirs atavistic impulses that harken back to times when human beings depended on hunting for food. You do not have to carry a rifle to recreate the inherent thrill of tracking, and the experience teaches kids the value of moving slowly when they want to observe wildlife. It also makes them appreciate the skills their ancestors had to develop in order to survive.

The shape, composition, and size of animal scat changes with each species. Deer leave piles of pellet-shaped scat. The scat of carnivores, such as fox, coyotes, and bobcats, often is composed of masses of hair from the prey animals they have eaten. Among the most interesting forms of scat are owl pellets, which are not droppings but instead are regurgitated pellets composed of the hair, bones, and tiny skulls of the snakes and rodents they have eaten. Look for these pellets underneath tree branches where the owls roost at night.

Unless you're familiar with animal sign, most tracks and scat will

---

Take That Animal Track Home

Did you know that kids can use plaster of paris molds to make castings of tracks for school projects? Kits for taking the impressions are sold in some outdoor stores. However, it is less expensive to buy a container of Hydrocal, a lightweight casting plaster, at a local hobby shop. Carry a little plastic bag of the Hydrocal on hikes. When you find a sharply defined animal track, mix the Hydrocal with a little water, pour it into the track, and wait 15 minutes for it to solidify. Lift it out and you will have a perfect mold of the track, which can be painted if the kids so desire.

be confusing. Buy a pocket guide, such as the *Pocket Naturalist*, which issues guides to fishes, stars, pond animals, and various other natural subjects, as well as to tracks and scat. They are published by Waterford Press (phone 800–434–2555) and widely distributed in bookstores and on the bookshelves of general stores in popular camping areas.

TREES AND WILDFLOWERS

With the exception of a few unique species, such as the Venus flytrap, which closes its petals upon unsuspecting insects, plants more or less stand in place and do not engage the curiosity of children as readily as animals do. But a parent's enthusiasms for any subject tends to rub off on his child, and if you demonstrate your passion for wildflowers, it won't be too long before your son's or daughter's sharp eyes are pointing out the stems of larkspur you've overlooked.

Make nature come alive by telling kids about plants that played a part in the lives of Native Americans, such as the reeds and cattails that grow along the edges of lakes. Indians ate the tubers of the cattails, which taste like cucumber. They also used the hollow stems of the reeds to breathe through while swimming underwater to sneak up and grab ducks for their dinner.

You can help nature come alive by telling kids about plants that play a part in the lives of animals, or sharing with your child an interest in wildflowers.

Look for "caches" of pine cones under exposed roots or the eves of rocks or downfall in evergreen stands. The piles are made by squirrels, which store the cones to eat during the lean months of winter. Show children how to tell the difference between pine and fir by feel: "prickly pine" has sharp needles; "friendly fir" has soft tufts that don't jab your hand.

Smooth-barked trees such as aspen, cottonwood, and birch readily show scars where animals have damaged them. Along rivers, many trees will have been gnawed upon by beavers, leaving the ground littered by wood chips. In the Rocky Mountains, you'll notice dark scars near eye level where elk have eaten the bark. Look for deep parallel cuts where bears have scraped their claws. Males of the deer family rub the velvet off their antlers against shrubs and the trunks of smaller trees before the fall rut. Sometimes, the bucks are so violent they break off many smaller branches. Examine the trunks to see if any hair adheres to them. Deer and elk hair is short, either gray or brown and quite brittle. Moose hairs are long and dark.

Don't neglect your children's education when it comes to poison ivy, poison oak, and poison sumac. Teaching them to identify these plants can save a lot of misery on down the trail.

STAR GAZING

Because the bright lights of cities obscure stars, urban children seldom see the gorgeous silver pepper night skies that can be observed from camp. Buy a star chart for your latitude and spend a few minutes before bedtime staring at the firmament. Have the kids see how many constellations they can find and show them how to pinpoint Polaris, the North Star, from the position of the Big Dipper. Explain to them how their ancestors used the position of the stars to keep their course when sailing the seas and wandering over uncharted lands.

Nature Photography

A good way of encouraging kids to take an interest in nature is to give them a camera. It need not be expensive. Even the disposable cameras that our children sometimes found in their Christmas stockings could take fairly good photographs, although both point-and-shoot and standard-sized 35mm cameras are obviously superior.

In camp, you can challenge children to take photographs of as many different animals and flowers as they can find. This makes a good vacation project and the pictures can be used for illustration when teachers ask for reports on what the children did during the summer. Obviously, a long lens of 100mm or more is helpful for wildlife photography, as is a macro lens for close-up pictures of bugs and flowers. But special lenses aren't really necessary. The rewards can sometimes be greater with ordinary lenses that don't magnify, because it makes the kids get closer to and become more familiar with their subjects. For example, my son was determined on one trip to take pictures of pronghorn antelope, which frequented the area where we camped but were skittish and usually seen at long ranges. He spent many hours stalking them with an old camera and a standard lens, finally getting a few pictures at 40 yards or so. The photos were nothing special, but the education was priceless, for over the course of several days, he learned far more about the daily habits and social behavior of pronghorns than most adults ever do. In addition, he learned the value of patience when studying wildlife and responsibility for taking good care of equipment, uncommon virtues among children his age.

One word of warning. Even careful kids will eventually drop cameras. Instruct them to wear the camera strap around their necks at all times. If they are going to get onto their knees to try to stalk closer to ground squirrels or other animals, make sure they have a pack or pocket where they can secure the camera, so it doesn't drag on the ground.

Star gazing is a first step toward learning wilderness navigation. When kids are old enough, further their education by teaching them to use a map and compass during day-hikes.

SPELLS CAST BY WATER

Children are drawn to water the way moths flutter to flame. They will hover at the bank of a stream or lake, wanting to get their feet wet, anxious to shiver from the cold, hoping someone will dare them to jump in.

Many times Gail and I made the mistake of planning hikes or other activities when all our children wanted to do was stay in camp to swim and build sand castles on the beach. Sand shovels and buckets should be part of every family camping trip that includes kids under the age of ten. So should inflatable air mattresses and inner tubes for swimming. Good swimmers can play Marco Polo, a water game of tag where the person who is "It" must keep his eyes closed. Whenever he shouts "Marco," the others must say "Polo." He has to keep swimming toward voices until he touches someone, who then becomes "It."

Older children will enjoy exploring the bottom of shallow areas with a mask and snorkel. A small collection net can add to their education by permitting close observation of aquatic insects, minnows, and frogs.

Another activity, suitable for all children past the toddler stage, is skipping stones. If you have never done this, then your own education has been sorely lacking. Pick small, flat stones and skim them just over the water with a quick snap of your wrist. Count how many

Camping close to water opens up a whole new world of possibilities. Try canoeing for a quiet, tranquil entry into the world of nature.

times they skip on the surface before sinking. Yes, it's a mindless pursuit that's beneficial only for developing coordination, but kids love it.

Because children seldom complain about eyestrain, it's easy to forget that their eyes need protection as much as yours do, particularly from the surface glare on the water. Polarized sunglasses not only eliminate the glare, but allow kids' eyes to penetrate the mirror of the surface to see fish, turtles, and other animals swimming underneath.

Boating is another activity children enjoy, more so if they are able to take part in it. Rowboats and canoes give them the opportunity to try their hands at oars and paddles. They will have much more fun turning circles with a paddle in their hands than sitting still in a motorboat.

Plan on packing life jackets and wading shoes as a matter of course during camping trips, and resign yourself to tossing away the blueprint of the day as soon as your children stick their feet into the water.

FISHING

It's been suggested that an angler's life passes through four stages: from the desire to catch any fish to catching as many as possible, to catching big fish, and ultimately, to pursuing only the most challenging fish.

Kids are content to stay at the second stage for a good long while, a lesson my son Tom and his cousin Brent taught me a long time ago. We were camping on a lake that had good early-morning bass fishing. Determined that the trip be successful, I had dragged both boys out of the tent at 5 A.M. and rowed the canoe while they cast small lures into the mist. Each of them caught a nice bass of 17 inches or so, but it was an icy morning and they could manage only a couple of casts before stuffing their hands into their pockets to warm up. Later in the afternoon I took them out again, to fish for perch with bobbers and worms in the sunshine. The dancing of the bobber, as fish lips nibbled at the worm, proved to be a moment of pure magic for the boys, as it had been for me when I was their age. It became clear they were having far more fun catching a basket of perch the size of their fingers than they had been getting one strike from a larger fish while they shivered.

If your family is new to fishing, I suggest purchasing a spincasting outfit with an enclosed-spool reel that releases line on the forward cast when you lift your thumb from a push-button. Don't buy the cheapest outfits; their half-life will be shorter than the duration of your vacation. A few bobbers, splitshots, and #6 and #8 bait hooks to hold the worm are all kids will need to catch the sunfish and perch that populate the weedy fringes of many warm-water lakes. Better quality spincast outfits will be okay for pitching lures to bass in the morning and evening. Spinning reels and bait-casting reels are more sophisticated tools that children can begin to master by the age of ten or so.

Many people consider fly fishing to be the most challenging and rewarding angling method. It differs from spincasting in that you cast the weight of the line by waving the rod back and forth, instead of casting a lure or bait that pulls line from the reel. The fly itself, which usually imitates an aquatic insect, weighs next to nothing. Fly fishing has a undeserved reputation for being elitist and difficult to master. Like other sports, it is easiest to learn through hands-on instruction. The basic skills are taught in outdoor schools sponsored by L.L. Bean as well as by many other organizations and fly shops throughout the country. L.L. Bean also offers a full line of fly fishing equipment. The *L.L. Bean Guide to Fly Fishing*, by Dave Whitlock, is an excellent primer on the sport.

Small panfish, such as bluegills and sunfish, take flies readily and offer children a stepping stone to the more challenging sport of fishing for trout. On northern trout streams, fly fishing is both the most enjoyable and often the most productive method. You'll also discover that it is much easier to release trout unharmed if you catch them with flies rather than with live bait, because the fish seldom inhale the fly into their gills or stomach. Since some fisheries can be easily damaged by killing your legal limit, or in some cases by killing even one fish, this is an important consideration.

All manners of angling offer a glimpse into the working order of nature that cannot be easily observed on land. Show your children how the lure they are using for bass imitates a small minnow or crawfish; on a trout stream, lift up stones to show them the aquatic insects the fishing fly duplicates. A rod is a key that opens the door to countless hours of enjoyment, but just as importantly, it is an educational tool that deepens children's appreciation and understanding of the outdoors.

Teaching kids to fish can be fun and exciting for both you and the child. For a child, the wild thrill of catching their first fish will last forever. For many of us, it is a memory that has led us to a lifetime in pursuit of this wonderful sport.

HIKING

Because hiking does not offer the instant gratification of kicking a soccer ball or hitting a baseball, some kids look upon it as more work than fun.

"Let's take a hike," is likely to be met with a pout or a heavenward roll of the eyes. "It's boring," son and daughter say in unison, and they have a point. Until you foster their interest in the relationships among plants and animals with the earth and turn their attention to the details of life along the trail, then one tree really is much like another, one bird pretty much indistinguishable from the next. I have found motivation to be more of a problem among kids who look to movies, television, and the computer for their entertainment, than among children who often have to make their own fun with sticks, stones, or whatever is at hand, but to some degree this is a problem all parents face.

Kids' attention spans are short. Trails tend to be long. In order to keep them interested, stop often. Pack a guidebook and explore the world at your feet. Look at a spider web, pick a feather for their hat, or examine the translucent curl of an old snakeskin. Explain how a snake peels out of its skin when it outgrows it and emerges in a colorful new one. Read the tracks in the mud by the creek. Find a woolly bear caterpillar and ask your children if they believe the popular myth about its stripes, that the wider the brown stripe is in the middle of the caterpillar, the milder the winter will be. If someone shakes his head no, say that it is often true, even though biologists have no idea why.

Start with short hikes, gradually increasing the distance as the children's strength and curiosity grow. Use an interesting destination as a motivational tool. Give them something they can visualize at the end of the trail—a waterfall, for example. But don't be disappointed if the cascade of water holds their attention for only a few moments. Kids are like cats. They aren't as interested in the view as they are in exploration. They like to climb on top of big rocks or walk across a log over a creek, not because it goes anywhere, but because it's there.

Having hobbies such as painting and photography helps. My son never needed more encouragement to hike than an assurance that he would be able to stop somewhere and bring out his sketchbook. Both children fished, so a mountain lake held a promise at the end of the trail.

We have found that you keep kids going by feeding their curiosity. You let them take turns using the walking stick with the bear bells, say.

Kids' attention spans are short, but trails tend to be long. Break up hikes by stopping often to explore the world at your feet. An appreciation of nature can begin small, with insects, amphibians, and plants that faster walkers tend to overlook.

Hobbies like painting, sketching, or photography help encourage kids to hike with the family.

When your five-year-old slows down, let her grasp the end of a stick or fishing rod case and tow her along behind you. Sing songs. A good sing-along is worth another mile of trail. When younger children tire, there's a point where it's easier to just pick them up and carry them.

One of the most important lessons we had to learn was that children who seem eager to hike one day may be adamantly against the idea the next. You must be sensitive to mood swings and keep a flexible schedule. A child who starts down the trail with a bad attitude will end up being carried a lot farther than one who starts his hike happy.

Front or backpack carriers are a must for babies, who are fascinated by changing scenery and make great little hikers, albeit ones who never put their feet on the ground. Choose a front carrier for infants, whose weak neck muscles can't support their heads in a backpack carrier. Toddlers can undertake short nature walks, but you'll wind up carrying them farther than they walk. Four- to six-year-olds can easily undertake hikes of a mile or two, but stamina doesn't really kick in for most kids until they are seven or eight. That's when they can begin to learn basic camping and hiking skills, as well. But keep in mind that their seemingly inexhaustible energy is still supported on short legs and they can tire on long hikes.

Teenagers who are asserting their independence present a different problem. They will balk at a suggestion simply because it's your suggestion. Let them enter the planning process of the hike with you, and if all else fails, have them invite a friend. A teen with a friend in tow will walk ten miles farther than one who must put up with the inferiority of adults all by himself.

A few special treats to dole out at critical junctures of the trail, like a stick of jerky or a bag of M&Ms, will go a long way toward making the hiking experience enjoyable for everyone.

Clothing for Family Hiking

Everyday athletic shoes are perfectly adequate for most hiking trails, especially for younger children, whose feet aren't supporting much weight. Trail shoes or light hiking boots offer more support and are better choices for walking over rough terrain. Consult the chart in the L.L. Bean catalog for recommendations; they offer footwear for everything from light dayhiking to backpacking under heavy loads. If you decide to mail-order, be ready to supply measurements of both feet to ensure getting a good fit.

Cotton socks are all right for short hikes during fair weather. But they offer little insulation and absorb perspiration, making them sticky, which leads to blisters on longer trails. Much better are sports-blend socks that have extra-thick cushioning at the heel, the ball of the foot, and around the toes. They are usually spun from polyester, nylon, and wool fibers, which wick sweat away from the skin, keeping feet dryer.

Serious hikers use a layering system of clothing. The *base layer*, worn next to the skin, is usually made of polypropylene or polyester—synthetic fabrics that wick perspiration away from the skin. *Outer layers* are composed of fibers that create dead air space for trapping body warmth. Fleece, pile, and wool are most popular. The last layer is the *shell,* meant to repel wind, rain, and snow. Shells that incorporate a microporous membrane, such as Gore-Tex, repel rain while allowing body moisture to escape. This allows the garment to "breathe," making it much more comfortable than "nonbreathable" polyurethane-coated nylon raingear. But it's also more expensive.

Do you really need to invest in specialized hiking apparel? Probably not, if you choose short hikes on bluebird days. Children don't sweat as much as adults do and really don't need to have clothing made of synthetic wicking fibers. Just make certain they wear loose clothing and bring a wool shirt or fleece jacket should the weather turn cool. Make sure each kid has a hat for sun protection, and in climates where

Be sure to pack sensibly and be prepared for various weather conditions—it will help make your hike safe and fun.

rain is likely, pack inexpensive ponchos. The farther you hike, the wilder the country is, or the worse the weather becomes, the more important it is to have good trail clothing. L.L. Bean offers a full line of apparel specifically designed for hiking. Choose bright colors for children. It will help you keep track of them should they stray off the trail.

On long hikes, daypacks or fanny packs are convenient for carrying extra clothes and basic survival gear. (Hint: Have kids bring their school backpacks on camping trips; they are perfectly adequate for light hiking.) Have each child carry these essentials in his or her pack:

- Warm clothing
- Rain poncho
- Trail snacks (power bar, granola bar, fruit)
- 1-liter container of water
- Whistle (in case a child becomes separated from parents or thinks he's in danger)

Survival Gear for Family Hiking

In addition to the kids' gear, at least one adult in the hiking party should pack a basic survival kit. Essentials include:

- Waterproof matches
- Solid fuel cubes or other fire-starting material
- Emergency space blankets (the kind that is sewn in the shape of a sleeping bag is the most efficient at conserving body warmth)
- Compass and map
- Sunscreen
- Insect repellent
- Small medical kit (many outdoor stores sell these, or they can be mail-ordered through L.L. Bean)
- A sheet of Spenco Second Skin and a square of moleskin for blisters
- Iodine tablets for water purification
- Toilet paper in reclosable plastic bag
- Flashlight with spare bulb and batteries (wrap the barrel with a few turns of electrical tape and a few turns of duct tape, for repairs)
- Signal mirror
- 20-foot roll of bright orange marking tape (to mark a trail in case you become lost)
- Knife
- Folded square of aluminum foil (for a dozen and one uses, including catching rainwater, cooking trout, covering a cup or pot, or even providing a heat-reflecting base where you can build an emergency fire in snow country)

Lost!

The Hug-A-Tree Program suggests guidelines for ensuring children's safety if they become separated from adults while hiking. The basic principles include:

1. At home, have your child walk across a piece of aluminum foil with the shoes he or she will hike in. Searchers can use the impression to identify tracks.

2. Give each child a large plastic trash bag to use as a poncho to shelter from the elements and a shrill whistle to signal for help.

3. Keep children oriented during hiking. Point out prominent landmarks and baselines, such as roads or rivers, as well as the position of the sun and what it means.

4. Assure kids that you won't be mad should they become separated from you. Some children have ignored the calls of searchers because they are afraid they will be scolded for getting lost.

5. Assure kids that many people will come looking for them if they get lost, so they should stay put rather than attempt to find their way back to the car.

6. Tell them to pick a big tree by the side of the trail and wait there. The tree grounds them, helps them avoid panic, and keeps them in one place.

7. Assure them that wild animals do not want to attack them. If they hear a noise, whether during the day or night, they are to shout at it and blow the whistle. If it's an animal, it will run away. If it's a person, they will be found.

8. Have children wear bright clothing and tell them to get in an open area near their tree and make themselves appear big for aerial rescue. Tell them to wave their clothing or packs should they hear an airplane.

In the unlikely event that your child does become lost, contact the sheriff's department immediately. Search and rescue teams, aided by tracking dogs, are so thorough and well trained that most kids will be found within 24 hours.

All of these items can be secured in a beltpack that is only 8 inches long by 4 inches deep. The extra pound is a small weight to carry for insurance against accidents.

BICYCLING

If you were to ask any kid between the ages of five and ten if he or she wanted to bring a bike on the camping trip, I believe the answer would be an unqualified "yes." Bikes are fun, not only on designated biking trails that skirt natural areas but also around campground loops and on the back roads that lead from camp to the nearest town. For several years, my daughter's attitude toward camping depended a great deal on whether her bicycle made the trip.

With bumper or roof racks, bikes are not as difficult to bring along as you might suspect, even for families with smaller vehicles. The Thule racks carried by L.L. Bean are among the finest made and are designed to fit nearly every car. However, bikes can cause problems. With bumper racks, you have to worry about parking; with roof racks, you scrape the bike against low tree branches. Theft also becomes a consideration. The car engine isn't as easy to check if you pack your bikes up front, and if you

want to bring a canoe or kayak, good luck.

During the several years our family carried bicycles, we compromised by taking only two and trading off in camp. The bikes made the cut because they added more to the enjoyment of the trip than the headache of packing them detracted from it. More recently, the pendulum has tipped in the other direction. It's a matter of family priorities.

Bikes offer kids and adults a great way to explore while camping. If you were to ask any child between the ages of 5 and 10 if he or she wanted to bring a bike on the camping trip, the answer would be an unqualified "yes."

REGIONAL ACTIVITIES

Berry picking and whale watching are among many attractions that can make a camping destination unique. They present parents with an excellent opportunity to bring a little education into the process of having fun. For example, when my brother and I climbed Maine's Mount Katahdin as youngsters, we were told by other hikers on the trail that if we made it to the top, we'd be

There's something magic about first light on the coast of Maine. On top of Cadillac Mountain in Acadia National Park, one gets to experience sunrise before anyone else in the country.

standing in the very place where the first rays of the rising sun touched our country. That lesson about the earth's rotation made a more lasting impression than any textbook illustration could possibly have done. We learned another lesson about sunspots and the collision of energy particles with atmospheric gases in Quebec when we observed a shimmering display of the northern lights.

Hunting for petosky stones along the shore of Lake Michigan was always a favorite activity. Each intricately fossilized stone told us a story of life in the epochs preceding human history.

Crabbing along the Oregon coastline introduced my children to the incredible wealth of life that exists beneath the churn of the sea. The cost of admission was only a few dollars for the rental of a crab trap. Although none of our crabs quite reached the minimum legal size, our original quest for dinner was quickly forgotten in Tom and Jessie's excitement as they hauled up the rope and then backed away wide-eyed as a dozen crabs scuttled free with their fighting claws extended.

A little research at the local library or an Internet search will point up regional opportunities in the area you plan to visit. Take advantage of these opportunities to add diversity and education to your camping trip.

PAINTING THE TOWN

It's a parent's dream to believe that children will be content to turn the pages of the book of nature for as long as they stay in camp. But for a kid who has been raised on theme parks, computer games, and team sports, an unvaried diet of hikes can get to be a little too much. Force-feeding them will only result in creating a lasting distaste for camping.

It may be a good idea on longer trips to indulge your kids' sweet tooth for less woodsy activities, such as miniature golf, water slides, or other roadside attractions near camp. I don't recommend doing this very often; after all, you *are* camping. But knocking a golf ball through a windmill once a week or going into town for an ice cream cone on a hot day helps break up routine and keeps kids motivated. Don't neglect local playhouses that cater to campers. Hotels in a few of the larger national parks offer nightly musical revues performed by college students; those I have attended were huge hits for adults and children alike.

RANGER TALKS

Every evening, campers at some of the larger national park campgrounds gather in front of a bonfire to listen to a ranger talk. Let's be honest. Some of these talks, though informative, will bore children out of their skulls. But others can prove interesting and even entertaining.

We took our children to a slide show one evening while camping in Glacier National Park. I was all set to doze through a carousel of picture postcards, and the ranger seemed suitably bland, a natty little fellow who, after introducing himself, apologized effusively for being new to the job and a little nervous.

"I love the way the ptarmigan changes its color to blend in with its environment, from the mottled grays of summer," he began—and here the slide of an appropriately muted bird appeared on the screen— "to the half-white of autumn"—click to a second slide— "to the snowy white of winter"—and another slide clicked on the screen, and it wasn't a grouse. It was a moose.

"Oh, I'm sorry," he said. "Somebody must have gotten into these slides and mixed up the order." He seemed so genuinely upset that no one dared to snicker. Next came a series of slides on the succession of summer flowers, ending with the park's most famous, "the creamy white stalks of bear grass." Click. It was a squirrel. There was a murmur of suppressed laughter. The ranger wiped his brow of sweat and his voice quavered as he struggled to continue.

By the third "mistake," the audience laughed outright. It was only then that the adults began to suspect that the person who had mixed up the slides might be the ranger himself. But he played his string out so adroitly, lulling us with his droning voice and a couple dozen slides in perfect order, that one began to doubt. Then the head of a rabbit popped up in the middle of a sequence on the park's "avian brothers" and the place exploded. I looked at the children. Their eyes were shining.

Whatever Glacier Park paid that ranger, it wasn't enough.

GAMES IN CAMP

When I asked my son, Tom, aged seven or eight at the time, what he enjoyed most when camping in Yellowstone Park, he unhesitatingly answered, "Whiffle ball." Games with a sponge rubber football came in a close second. A year or two later, Frisbee golf in a field next to the campground was the winner. Dried-up buffalo chips were the holes!

These weren't the answers I wanted to hear, but they prove that camping is more than just nature worship, even for a kid who loves to fish and paint wildlife.

Hacky sack isn't as exciting as a ball game, but it has the advantage of requiring no open spaces and doesn't disturb neighbors. Board games take little space in the car and also are great camp favorites. There's something about sitting around the picnic table on a warm night, playing a game of Clue or Monopoly by lantern light, that makes it much more appealing than it is at home. A magnetic chess and checkers board serves double duty—fun in camp and also on the road. Bring a couple of decks of cards and a card game book for a change of pace.

Jacks and marbles, two games today's kids may have never heard of, offer great camp entertainment. And they can be played in the dirt, which is the all-time favorite medium for any kids' game. As a bonus, they take up absolutely no space in the car.

My wife's favorite game is charades. It gets everyone involved, is a great ice breaker if you have visitors in camp, and is particularly dramatic when performed in the play of shadows and light created by the evening campfire.

LEISURE TIME IS PART OF CAMPING, TOO

Our government likes to say that Americans today enjoy more free time than their parents had. As a father, I don't buy that. In fact, it seems to me that our lives, both at work and at home, have never been more rigidly ordered, and if we don't work as many hours on the job, we more than make up for it by carting kids to and from all of their school activities. And at home, kids seldom just walk outside to play anymore. Free time is structured. They even have to make phone calls to arrange play dates.

So I think it's important to remember that a camping trip is, after all, a vacation. There's nothing wrong with a spending a day reading or lazing around, while the children are left to their own devices. Just use your judgment and set boundaries for their play or times when they have to return to the campsite.

Relaxing is a part of camping, too.

It is important to remember that camping means vacation time. Even kids need "down time." There is nothing wrong with spending an afternoon writing in a journal, reading, or lazing around.

CHAPTER
9

Bugs, Bears, and Rainy Day Blues

"[T]he musquetoes continue to infest us in such manner that we can scarcely exist; for my own part I am confined by them to my bier (netting) at least ¾ ths of my time. My dog even howls with the torture . . ."

JOURNAL ENTRY OF CAPTAIN MERIWETHER LEWIS
AT THE GREAT FALLS OF THE MISSOURI RIVER, JULY 15, 1806

Nearly two centuries have passed since Lewis's "musquetoes" brought his party to the brink of madness above the falls. In that time, grizzly bears have been driven from the Missouri River Breaks to a last stronghold in the mountains and the wild bison have left only the odd skull to mark their passing. But the region's most numerous denizens remain in force.

When my brother walks from our tent to the bank of the Missouri, a cloud of vampires rings his head. Attracted by the carbon dioxide fumes that escape his mouth and the odor of lactic acid given off by his slightest exertion, the halo they form pulses in anticipation.

Fortunately, a great deal of the misery that biting and stinging insects cause can be prevented. The easiest way is to avoid camping in low-lying country near ponds and streams where the insects breed, especially during the first hot weeks of summer. If you time family vacations during spring or late summer, just before school starts back up, cooler nights will dampen the insects' enthusiasm. But even in places where bugs are numerous, they need not ruin a trip, as long as you know how to repel their attacks.

MOSQUITOES AND BLACK FLIES

Mosquitoes and black flies comprise the one-two punch that KO's more summer outings than the rest of the creeping, buzzing, and crawling kingdom combined. Mosquitoes breed in still water and are most active in the mornings and evenings. Black flies, along with their pinpoint cousins, gnats and no-see-ums, are drawn to dark colors and swarm about the face, having a fondness for eye secretions. Black flies breed in faster currents and are most bothersome during daylight hours.

The first line of defense against both species is loose-fitting, tightly woven clothing. Use rubber bands on kids' pants and shirt cuffs to keep insects from getting underneath their clothes. The best insect repellent is DEET (a chemical compound that does not so much repulse insects as confuse their sensors, causing them to stay in a holding pattern rather than land and bite). Most people can apply DEET liberally during camping vacations and experience no harmful side effects. However, long exposure has been known to cause rashes, eye and sinus problems, headaches, and insomnia. DEET also can remove the plastic coating from fly lines and eat holes through plastic tents, women's nylon stockings, and even the upholstery of your car.

DEET repellents are sold in cream, liquid, and aerosol forms. Those that have a 30- to 35-percent solution are recommended for adults. Children under two should not be exposed to DEET. Older kids can use a 6- to 10-percent solution, which loses its effectiveness and must be reapplied more often than higher concentrations. Don't apply the repellent next to their eyes, mouth, or any cuts.

Natrapel, Avon's Skin-So-Soft, and other products that contain citronella repel mosquitoes and black flies somewhat less effectively than DEET, and also must be reapplied more often. The up side is that citronella, a plant derivative, is easier on the skin.

In severely infested areas, consider spraying your clothing, *not your skin,* with permethrin, which is sold under several trade names as an arthropod or tick repellent. It is an insecticide that kills bugs on contact, but it is not harmful to children or adults.

Nearly all modern tents come with a mesh mosquito netting. Some, but not all, have a fine enough grid to repel no-see-ums. If you live in the Northeast, it's important to check this feature before purchase. During a camping trip to Prince Edward Island when I was a child, I spent a miserable night being chewed on by insects no one else was aware of. My mother, who was better covered up by her sleeping bag, couldn't understand why I was doing so much complaining. She rose in the morning to find my scalp covered with hundreds of crimson spots left by the bites of no-see-ums. To be doubly certain of keeping these microscopic pests out of your hair, spray the netting at the mouth of the tent with permethrin.

A large screen bug tent offers campers sanctuary from biting insects at a modest price. People who are sensitive to the buzzing of insects as well as their bite might be happy they made the investment. Lighting a citronella candle will help keep at bay the few mosquitoes that manage to fly inside the screen when the door is unzipped, but take the precaution of placing the candle inside a globe to prevent accidents. Vaporizing mats containing a pyrethroid substance also are effective deterrents when used inside tents and screen houses. Smoldering mosquito coils look neat and kids like to light them, but mostly they just raise an ineffectual smoke.

Treatment

Because humans build up a certain amount of immunity from mosquito and fly bites, children are often the most affected. Itching can be soothed by ice packs and topical application of Calamine lotion or over-the-counter steroid creams. People who are hypersensitive to mosquito bites can obtain more powerful prescription steroids. Oral antihistamines also help.

LARGER BITING INSECTS

Horseflies, deer flies, and stable flies are not easily deterred by repellents. They tend to be attracted to foods, brightly colored clothing, and perfumes. Swatting at flies, whose multifaceted eyes are attuned to movement, only draws the attention of others which may not have otherwise spotted you. There is really no deterrent for these pests except to keep food put away, dress in muted tones, camp in windy areas, and otherwise try to avoid them.

Mosquitoes and black flies comprise the one-two punch that KO's many summer outings. The first line of defense is loose-fitting clothing they can't bite through, natural repellents, and repellents containing DEET.

Treatment

Treat fly bites exactly as you would mosquito bites.

STINGING INSECTS

The same preventive measures for deer and horseflies also work for bees, wasps, yellow jackets, and hornets. Keep in mind that bees are irritable on cool, overcast days and are attracted to yellow and blue colors. Avoid nests and beware of swarms that fly in a straight line, since they are likely returning to a hive and can be aggressive.

Meat-loving yellow jackets can be particularly bothersome in some campgrounds. If there are only a few of them around, the old backyard barbecue trick of filling a dish with sugar water and setting it away from the picnic table to draw the yellow jackets may work. But when there are a lot of them, the sugar water merely acts as a soup kitchen for the masses and you will soon find the hangers-on orbiting your stove, sipping spilled soft drinks from the table top, and standing on your fork as you lift it to eat.

Children, who are naturally more careless about where they place their hands than adults, are most likely to be stung. In a couple of campgrounds I have visited, finding a spot to eat a peaceful meal was no easy chore. A screen tent would have been the solution.

Treatment

Immediately check any child who has been stung to see if the stinger is still embedded. Scrape the site with a dull knife to remove it. Sometimes you can pick a stinger out with tweezers, but take care not to squeeze it and release more venom. Wash the wound, then apply ice or rubbing alcohol to ease the sting. Traditional bug-bite treatment used for mosquitoes will help dull the pain. Aspirin or ibuprofen also may help.

Allergic reactions to bee, wasp, yellow jacket, and hornet stings can be extremely serious. Children are probably at risk if they experience dizziness, rash, difficult breathing, a swollen tongue, or vomiting the first time they are stung. If someone in your family is allergic, make certain you purchase a beesting kit for warm-weather camping. It includes an epinephrine self-injector, which causes airways to expand and keeps heartbeat regular until you can reach a hospital.

TICKS

The deer tick that carries Lyme disease is a parasite that feasts on the blood of its namesake host. Because its bite can be serious, it's a good idea to take precautions, especially in some Eastern Seaboard regions where whitetail deer and ticks are very common. To deter ticks, use a combination of DEET applied to skin and permethrin sprayed onto clothing. On hikes, avoid tall grass and make your children wear long pants and long-sleeved shirts (put rubber bands over the cuffs to keep them tightly closed). Stick to light colors for clothing, so that you can spot any ticks that cling to the fabric (remember that some ticks, including the darkly colored deer tick, are no larger than a freckle or the period on a printed page). Check your body and comb your hair a couple of times each day. To remove a tick, grasp it with tweezers close to your skin and pull straight out. Don't crush the tick's body; that will increase the chance of infection. Make sure the tick's head and mouth parts are not left in the skin.

Treatment

Most people who contract Lyme disease develop a bull's-eye-like rash around the tick bite within 3 to 30 days after being bitten. Other early symptoms include fatigue, fever, and headache. Pinpoint-size blood spots that erupt on the wrists, ankles, the palms of the hands, and the soles of the feet, and which are accompanied by fever and chills, point to Rocky Mountain spotted fever, another tick-related disease. Both can be cured with antibiotics. But arthritis and heart problems can result for those who go untreated, so make certain any family members who exhibit symptoms see a doctor.

SPIDERS AND SCORPIONS

Female black widow spiders and brown recluse spiders inflict serious bites that warrant medical attention. Black widows are large, round-bodied, shiny black spiders. The female can be

Follow this person's example and keep your outdoor experience pleasurable by taking extra care in areas with biting and stinging insects. There are plenty of things we can do to avoid them.

identified by the small orange or red hourglass on her abdomen. Brown recluse spiders are light-colored, with a darker, violin-shaped marking on their backs. Both are widespread species, although the brown recluse spins its web mainly south of the Mason-Dixon line.

Several species of scorpions inhabit our southern states. The sting from most of them is a little more painful than a bee sting and should be treated the same way. The only scorpion that poses any serious danger is the bark scorpion of the Sonoran Desert. The bark scorpion is yellow or brown, with dark brown stripes down its back and has a large knob at the base of its stinger.

Take precautions to avoid contact with spiders and scorpions by shaking out your shoes and clothing before dressing each morning, and shaking out your sleeping bag before turning in at night. Don't let the kids walk about barefoot and leave every stone *unturned.*

Treatment

Because the bite of black widow spiders is initially painless, it's important to recognize the symptoms, which include sweating and cramping of muscles near the site of the bite within 15 minutes to one hour after envenomation. The black widow's bite is almost never fatal, but apply a cold pack to the bite area, and, to be on the safe side, seek medical attention. The bite of the brown recluse spider also may be painless, but usually it hurts like hell. Swelling at the site follows rapidly. There's nothing you can do in the field but swallow aspirin, apply an ice pack, and head for the nearest hospital.

The sting of the bark scorpion carries a neurotoxic venom similar to that of cobras and coral snakes, although not so powerful. Most adults experience nothing more than moderate pain that fades after a few hours. Children and the elderly, or anyone who has high blood pressure, may be more at risk and can experience a variety of reactions, including tingling, involuntary muscle twitching, rapid pulse, and soaring blood pressure. They also may have difficulty breathing. Apply ice packs for the pain and seek medical attention immediately.

POISONOUS SNAKES

Having been fascinated by snakes since childhood, I am often appalled at public ignorance and animosity toward these beautiful creatures. The vast majority of snakes you will encounter are entirely harmless. In all the years I've been camping, only once have I come across a poisonous snake in the vicinity of a campground. It was a rare Massassauga rattler. Like others of its kind, it made no attempt to rattle and probably could not have been induced to bite me unless I had picked it up with my bare hands.

The four varieties of North American poisonous snakes are easily identified and avoided.

Copperheads and water moccasins are stout-bodied snakes with prominent, triangular heads and an hourglass pattern across their backs. Copperheads seldom exceed three feet in length and have alternating bands of light copper and darker brown. They are commonly found in fields and hardwood forests throughout much of the East, Southeast, and Midwest. Watch for them near stone walls and on rocky ledges. The copperhead's southern cousin, the water moccasin, is a larger, heavier snake. It is much darker and when it is wet from swimming (it frequents swamps and river basins) it can appear to be nearly black. The inside of the water moccasin's mouth is white—hence, the moniker "cottonmouth."

Rattlesnakes are distinguished by large, triangular heads and the segmented, fingernail-like substance that comprises the rattle at the end of their bodies. They inhabit many parts of the country and range in size from the diminutive pygmy rattlesnake, which seldom exceeds 18 inches, to the massive eastern diamondback, which can reach eight feet in length and sports hinged fangs nearly an inch long.

Coral snakes are smaller, southern reptiles, easily distinguished by their bright, alternating bands of red, yellow, and black. They are members of the cobra family and have a highly toxic venom, but are inoffensive and seldom bite unless roughly handled.

Contrary to popular belief, poisonous snakes are not aggressive toward humans. However, they sometimes strike when too closely approached or stepped upon. Simply give them a wide berth and continue down the trail. Since snakes are largely nocturnal during hot weather, it's a good idea to use a flashlight when walking about camp at night. Keep children away from brushy areas and if rattlesnakes or copperheads are common in the area, have them refrain from lifting up stones or climbing among rocky ledges.

Treatment

The best first aid for snakebite is a set of car keys. If someone is bitten, keep the wounded limb below heart level and drive to a hospital. There's no need for panic. Fewer than 15 people die of snakebite in the United States annually, and of those who do succumb, many were bitten while handling snakes or otherwise putting themselves in harm's way.

POISONOUS PLANTS

Amongst my earliest memories is the voice of my mother calling to warn me to "stay out of the poison ivy." At least once a summer her forearms would erupt in boils the size of nickels, probably as a result of handling clothes my brother and I had dirtied while playing outdoors. For people who are sensitive to *urushiol,* the chemical compound that is found in the leaves, stems, and roots of poison ivy, poison oak, and poison sumac, a camping trip to nearly any destination within the United States can result in a souvenir rash that itches for days.

The first of two keys to prevention is identification. Both poison ivy and its western cousin, poison oak, are characterized by *usually* having three shiny leaflets on each stem. The leaves of ivy are pointed; those of oak are lobed. Both plants can grow as ground cover, a trailing shrub, or a rope-like, woody vine. In addition, poison oak is often seen as a taller, standing shrub. Poison sumac is a swamp-loving, rangy shrub that grows to 15 feet and has between 7 and 13 smooth-edged leaflets per stem.

The second step to prevention is the careful handling and prompt washing of shoes and clothes that may be contaminated. Sticks and other objects your dog drags out of the woods can pass on the rash, as can the hair of the dog itself. It's also important to be careful when

---

The Mud Pack Cure

Barrier creams that prevent urushiol from penetrating the skin are available without prescription in drugstores and outdoor equipment shops. Ivy Block, Ivy Shield, and Stokogard Outdoor Cream come in lotion form; when applied, they dry into a clay-like coating. They have been proven to be effective, but can be uncomfortable and must be applied every four hours or so to ensure protection. Daily use around the campground may be impractical; however, they could be a godsend for hikers who bushwhack into poison ivy- or poison oak-infested forests.

---

gathering firewood, because burning the stems or leaves of ivy releases urushoil into the smoke. My wife once contracted a rash of poison oak on her feet after hanging her socks to dry over a fire in California's Sequoia National Park.

The "active ingredient" of poison ivy has a long shelf life. Handling clothing or camping gear can result in a rash several years after the oil came in contact with the object.

Treatment

If you think your children may have brushed against poison ivy, wash affected areas promptly with rubbing alcohol and then stick them in the shower; there is some evidence that soap spreads the rash, so have them wash first with water only. Redness and swelling typically appear a day or two after initial contact. The seeping blisters that erupt in severe cases don't contain urushiol, are not contagious, and the rash usually subsides within a couple of weeks. Some relief can be found in over-the-counter topical steroid creams, such as Cortaid and Lanacort. Antihistamines reduce itching, as do oatmeal baths. Running hot water over the rash often produces temporary relief. Cortisone shots and prescription oral corticosteroids offer the only truly effective treatment and work best when taken at the outset of the rash.

BEARS AND OTHER BUMPS IN THE NIGHT

Bears are a lot more prevalent in campfire tales than they ever have been around the campfire itself. Nonetheless, in some campgrounds they can be a nuisance. It may be entertaining to watch a man engage in a tug of war with a bear over

While it is true that bears are a lot more prevalent in campfire tales than they have ever been around the campfire itself, it is important to heed bear warnings by taking appropriate precautions to avoid an encounter.

a Virginia smoked ham, as I did when we camped in the Smoky Mountains many years ago, but such encounters often result in the destruction of the bear.

Bears will do most anything to get food, including, in a few areas, breaking into cars. Fortunately, the latter occurrence seems to be a California curse—outside Yosemite and Sequoia National Parks, bears usually show more respect for the automobile industry. In fact, in most bear country the best way to avoid having your camp raided is by locking all food and cooking gear *inside* the vehicle. Campers at walk-in sites should store their food in metal strongboxes provided at the site or hang it from a tree. To make a "bear hang," tie a rock to a strong cord and toss it over a branch 12 to 15 feet overhead, then attach the food bag where the cord was tied to the rock and pull it up. The food bag should be looped over the tree limb at least ten feet away from the trunk, to keep bears from climbing the tree and knocking it down.

Most bears will flee from hikers, but a few will become aggressive when they are surprised at short range. Stay on established paths and don't let kids run ahead or lag behind. Misguided by dozens of Saturday morning cartoons, children tend to think of bears as warm, fuzzy animals. You must teach them that bears can be dangerous.

Black bears (which also come in shades of brown, red, and even blond) live throughout the U.S. The much larger grizzly, distinguished by its dished snout and exaggerated shoulder hump, is confined to the northern region of the Rocky Mountains. Grizzlies are much more likely to react to intrusion into their territory by attacking. In places where they are common, such as Yellowstone and Glacier National Parks, it's wise to hike in large parties. Reveal your presence to any bears within earshot by singing, talking, or rattling bear bells. My son and his friend Carly once serenaded our party during a long hike into the backcountry of Glacier, singing, among many off-pitch Beatles tunes, all 100 verses of "A Hundred Bottles of Beer on the Wall." The adults winked at each other because the children were small and it seemed so charming, but at the same time I was mighty glad their vocal cords were getting some exercise, because the trail was deserted and the country exuded that profound northern silence so deeply resonant of bear.

Most bears will flee from hikers, but a few will become aggressive if they are surprised at short range. Stay on established trails and let bears know of your presence by talking loudly or using bear bells.

Sows with cubs are the most dangerous bears to cross. Back away slowly from confrontations and drop a piece of gear (not food) to try to distract them. Climb a tree if one is handy, pushing your children up above you. Don't look the bear in the eye; that is considered to be a threatening posture. Many bears bluff a charge without making contact. If a bear does attack, drop to the ground and assume a fetal position to protect your vital organs; lock your hands behind your head to protect your neck. Cover kids with your body to protect them. Grizzlies often will content themselves with batting you about a little, until they feel the threat has been eliminated, then leave.

On rare occasions, bears have attacked humans in tents or actively stalked them on back-country trails. Such animals are not defending cubs or territory and playing dead won't do you any good. Fight back against them with anything you can reach.

In recent years, cayenne pepper sprays have become very popular among backcountry en-thusiasts. They have been shown to deter determined bear charges, but must be used prop-erly. If you purchase a canister, make certain you read the instructions thoroughly and test it before use.

MOUNTAIN LIONS

Twenty years ago, a serious discussion of mountain lions would have smacked of sensational-ism in a camping book. *Felix concolor* kept to himself and like so many things we fear but do not understand, the elusive cat was known by many names—puma, painter, panther, cougar, catamount. But a recent surge in population, coupled with humans moving into the fringes of its mountain strongholds, has resulted in hundreds of confrontations over the past decade or so, a handful of which have ended in human deaths.

Most mountain lion attacks target small women and children. I know of only two instances of lions attacking humans in organized campgrounds: at Lake McDonald Campground in Glacier National Park and Swift Dam Campground near Depuyer, Montana. Confrontations are much more likely along backcountry trails. Southern California has probably recorded the most incidents.

Make children walk between adults while negotiating dense cover in mountain lion coun-try. Cats are reluctant to attack humans head on, so in a confrontation face the cat, pick up smaller children, make yourself appear as threatening and large as possible, and use any means to fight back and discourage the attack.

Bear in mind that the vast majority of people who live among mountain lions never even see one. Don't be discouraged from camping or hiking among the mountains and canyons they prowl. You are still much more likely to be struck by lightning than by fang or claw.

THE RAIN

A raindrop has no teeth to bare, no proboscis to suck your blood, and no stinger at the base of its abdomen. Yet no animal or insect can so abruptly bring a camping trip to a halt.

Many campers are driven home by rain, but I prefer to look at it as God's way of telling a family to relax and spend a little more time in each other's company. Rain lends a sense of insularity and camaraderie to those who huddle underneath a tarp or spreading spruce, and some of my fondest memories of camp life are of card games, charades, or Trivial Pursuit played out under the shelter of a rain fly. Sitting with a book and a tin cup of brandy under the lip of a tarp and poking at a good fire that won't let a little water dampen its spirit; that's living.

But camping in rain, when you are unprepared for it, can be the most miserable of experiences. As a father who has both won and lost more than a few duels with our atmosphere's darker moods, I can offer a few suggestions that work under *most* conditions.

Pitch your tent on either flat or slightly sloping ground that offers good drainage and face the door opening away from prevailing winds. Use a plastic ground cloth underneath the tent and, in country where daily rains are likely, spread out a second ground cloth inside on the floor of the tent. Place a square of Astroturf just outside the door under the awning; have the kids wipe their shoes there (or remove them and change into camp slippers) to keep from tracking mud into the tent. If you don't have an awning, place the Astroturf inside the doorway and keep bedding away from the entrance. Close all windows and zippers tightly before leaving camp.

The most popular and least expensive rain flies come with four poles that poke through steel grommets at the corners, plus one adjustable center pole. Each corner pole is staked down with two guy ropes and two tent pegs. Try to pick a campsite that has several trees spaced ten feet or more apart from each other so that you can tie off a couple corners of the fly to the trunks. That way, you won't have to clutter the ground with as many guy ropes. I've seen kids trip over them while engaged in horseplay. Erect the tarp to cover only half the picnic table, leaving enough space for a few chairs, while still providing a surface to cook on at the table's sheltered end. This placement also allows the cook to stand underneath the tallest part of the fly, where he doesn't get dripped on or have to duck his head. Another solution is to pitch the fly over a folding camp table at the periphery of the site and use the picnic table in fair weather.

L.L. Bean offers several advanced fly designs that stand up to wind and slanting rain better than the conventional type found in sporting goods stores. They are worth considering, especially if you do a lot of camping along the Pacific Coast or in other areas where blue skies are the exception rather than the rule.

Before leaving camp for the afternoon, spread an extra ground tarp over firewood or other gear and make sure to loosen the guy ropes on the rain fly. If you expect much wind, drape the fly over the table to keep it from tearing loose.

For walking around in the rain, slip a pair of thin rubber overshoes over your children's shoes. They won't stand up to everyday use, but cost pennies, take up no space in the car, and offer the best way I know of keeping kids' footwear dry. In a pinch, you can step into a couple of plastic grocery bags and tie the cut-out handles across your ankles.

Prolonged downpours are hard to deal with no matter how well you have prepared the campsite. These are good days to go to town or somewhere else the rain can't find you. When we camped in Michigan, my mother and father reserved trips to the Hartwick Pines State Park for overcast days, where we could stroll underneath the protective

Don't let a little rain dampen your spirits. Good-quality raingear can't change the weather, but it will permit you to enjoy what might be a miserable day without it.

needle canopy of ancient trees. Visits to the Cherry Bowl Drive-In Theater near Beulah were another treat on iffy evenings. My father would pull on his waders for fishing after we had parked, then disappear over the hill into the river bottom while we watched the latest Disney adventure. By the time Dad climbed back up to the car, I would have fallen in love all over again with Hayley Mills, and only the silver sides of trout hanging from his wader belt could tear my eyes from the screen.

Today, of course, the Cherry Bowl Drive-In is just another piece of American nostalgia, but near any place you camp there will be natural history museums or other attractions that are perfect for a rainy evening.

Rainy nights can be wonderful or miserable, depending upon your tent's ability to shed water. The canvas tents my generation grew up with formed beads of water if you pressed your finger against them during a rain. Holes also were a problem, caused mainly by improper care and mold. One summer, an old German immigrant brought me inside his striped tent at Burton Landing in Michigan and showed me where he had stitched long threads to the edges of the holes. The threads extended down toward the floor, where he had tied them together over the mouth of a galvanized water pail. He said the raindrops ran down the threads and collected in the pail, leaving his cot dry. It was hard to believe such a simple trick would work. But it did work, and so for years thereafter, the interiors of our tents were spider-webbed by strands of sewing thread. How I loved to lie in my sleeping bag and watch raindrops run down the threads in the beam of a flashlight.

Modern tents don't leak nearly so bad as the old canvas ones, which makes family camping in the rain a less trying experience. Rain falling on nylon doesn't have quite the same quality of sound as it does on canvas. But the effect is not lost and in my experience, nothing compares with the patter of soft rain to make a person feel at peace with the world, to snuggle down in the sleeping bag a little further and drift to sleep on the rise and fall of nature's most soothing melody.

CHAPTER
10

Health and Safety

"Who would not give a trifle to prevent what he would give a thousand words to cure?"

EDWARD YOUNG

We camp to get away from the grid of urban sprawl, to be near what's left of God's glory: peaceful water, a cheerful campfire, the sunset on the mountain's peak. Lulled into a sense of complacency by nature's placid veneer, it's easy to forget that the crystal current of an alpine stream hosts a parasite that can make our stomachs knot in agony, or that hiking to a high pass can lead to altitude sickness.

Because I write a health and safety column for *Field&Stream* and talk to physicians and accident victims on a regular basis, I tend to be overly sensitive to the perils of the trail. The fact is that most camping mishaps are minor: a sprained ankle, a superficial sunburn, a stomach ache from eating too many hot dogs and S'mores. But a few can result in serious injury or sickness. For this reason, it is important to understand symptoms of illnesses, as well as basic first aid treatments. It's equally important to know how to recognize dangerous situations and prevent injuries from occurring.

LIGHTNING

Lightning kills more Americans than all other natural disasters combined. Don't be misled into second-guessing your safety by counting seconds between lightning strikes and peals of thunder. If the family is canoeing a lake when dark clouds begin to gather, get to shore immediately. If you're along a trail, discard metal objects such as backpack frames or graphite fly rods and seek shelter among bushes or rocks of uniform size. Stay off ridge tops and away from tall, tapering trees. Don't huddle in damp depressions or caves, which can conduct ground electricity from a nearby lightning strike. Squat with your feet together or sit on a foam pad or other nonconductive material to insulate your body from ground shock.

Parents should not group together with their children as a storm approaches. It's safer for each to take a child and split up. Stay in eye contact, however, so that if one group is struck, at least one adult can begin to administer emergency aid.

Serious burns are rare among lightning victims; the danger is that the electrical charge (lightning can galvanize the human body with 100 million volts of electricity) will short-circuit the respiratory system, which can lead to cardiac arrest. If several people have been struck, attend to those who appear dead first. Promptly administer rescue breathing and/or cardiopulmonary resuscitation (CPR) and don't be discouraged by the ashen visage of the victim. Many people who have survived lightning strikes have shown no signs of life for up to an hour during CPR, before they resumed breathing on their own. Send a member of your party for help and don't give up until it arrives.

ALTITUDE SICKNESS

One in four people who live at sea level will experience symptoms of acute mountain sickness (AMS) by climbing or driving to 7,000 feet, the average altitude of campgrounds in Yellowstone Park. At 10,000 feet, more than half of the visitors accustomed to sea level will become ill. AMS is brought about by the decrease in atmospheric pressure at higher elevations, which reduces the pressure that drives oxygen across the gas/blood membranes in the lungs. It is sometimes called "drunkard's syndrome," because as the saturation of oxygen in the blood falls, the victim can undergo mood changes, specifically lassitude and an inability to think clearly or walk a straight line. Common symptoms include nausea, dizziness, pounding headaches, and impaired breathing.

Susceptibility to AMS is not correlated with sex, age, or level of fitness. You or your spouse may suffer while the children remain fine. But the opposite can happen just as easily, so keep an eye out for symptoms. You can't depend on victims to articulate their illness, regardless of their maturity.

To avoid problems, acclimate to altitude by climbing no more than 2,000 feet in a day, and if you fly from sea level to higher altitude, rest in town for a day before driving any higher. For some reason, hikers who climb several hundred feet higher than their camp and return to lower elevation to sleep are less susceptible to AMS than those who camp at the highest altitude they have reached. That is something to consider if you have driven to a high elevation camp. Eating carbohydrates such as pasta may help stave off AMS by increasing carbon dioxide levels in the body.

Although this young person is enjoying her hike near Washington's Mount Rainier, one in four people will experience symptoms of acute mountain sickness (AMS) when driving or hiking above 7,000 feet.

Use aspirin (acetaminophen for small children) to relieve headaches, but for more serious symptoms, a prompt retreat to lower elevation is the only cure.

BURNS

Burns are among the most frequent camping injuries, especially among children, who are naturally more careless than adults. Improper handling of stoves and lanterns, starting fires by dousing wood with gasoline, and tripping and falling into campfires are among the most common causes of burns during camping vacations. You also have to keep kids back from campfires that spit sparks, which can cause corneal burns of the eye. Other burns are caused by steam and hot water, usually spilled when someone picks a pot up by a hot wire handle and suddenly drops it.

Backpacking stoves that have the fuel canister mounted directly under the burner can become too hot when you set them in holes or between rocks to cook out of the wind. The heat buildup can blow the pressure cap, resulting in a jet of flame. Kerosene heaters used to warm tents are extremely dangerous, not only because they can catch the tent fabric on fire, but because they emit toxic fumes when accidentally tipped over.

The rule of thumb for anyone whose clothing has caught fire is stop, drop, and roll. Smother flames with a sleeping bag or blanket and quickly remove jewelry, wristwatches, and any burned clothing that can retain heat (polypropylene and fleece are notorious in this respect). For skin burns, reduce the temperature of the affected area for up to 10 minutes with cool (but not ice-cold) water, either by rinsing or using wet rags. Cleanse the wound with boiled water that has been allowed to cool and dress the burn by applying an antibiotic ointment such as silver sulfadiazine (Silvadene). Wrap with a snug, sterile bandage or T-shirt. Elevate a burned arm or leg and leave the bandage in place while driving to a hospital.

Chemical burns caused by spilled battery acid during improper use of jumper cables—and what camper has not had to use jumper cables at some point in his or her life—are extremely serious. Wash battery acid burns with copious amounts of water. If the eyes have been splattered, remove contact lenses (if present) and flush the eyes under running water for 20 minutes.

Burns often are much more serious than they initially appear to be. Full-thickness burns—those that go deeper than the dermis layer underlying the skin—may not hurt because nerve endings have been destroyed. Play it safe by seeking a medical opinion if you have any doubt about the severity of a burn.

NEAR-DROWNING ACCIDENTS

Except for car crashes, drowning is the most common cause of accident-related death among children under 14. Parents must be extremely vigilant when camping near water. Many children balk at wearing life jackets ("The other kids don't have to wear them" is a line I must have used on my mother 100 times, and which has come back to haunt me in the voices of my children), but they are the first line of defense against drowning. You simply have to put your foot down until kids become good swimmers and know better than to play near banks of deep, swift-flowing rivers. Even small streams can be dangerous if kids slip and hit their heads on rocks. Another common cause of drowning is diving head-first into shallow water off docks and injuring the spinal cord.

The first rule of life saving is not to drown yourself. Victims thrash about and in their panic try to climb on top of would-be rescuers. It's always safest to throw a rope to someone in trouble or reach out to them with a long stick. If that isn't possible and the victim has submerged in deep water, swim out to them underwater. Turn the person so that he faces away from you, then raise his head out of water by lifting him under the armpits. Place your hand under his jaw and level out his body near the surface. Then reach one arm around and across his chest, with his head under your chin, and swim sidestroke to shore.

Don't worry about trying to get water out of the victim's stomach or lungs. Focus instead on clearing the airway and getting the victim to breathe. If the victim is in cardiac arrest, immediately start CPR and continue until help has arrived. Some children have been known to live after an hour's submersion in cold waters. It is believed that their small bodies cool so

Kids may balk at the idea of wearing a personal flotation device, but it is the only safe way to play or camp near water. If the life jacket fits properly, most children will forget they are wearing one.

rapidly that their brains are somehow protected from injury due to oxygen loss. Don't give up on them.

Remember that children look at water as a big playground. By keeping careful watch over them, you can prevent most accidents.

HYPOTHERMIA

It does not take extreme cold for a person to become hypothermic. Any combination of cool temperature, wind, becoming wet or drenched with perspiration, or being unable to move due to injury, can put a hiker at risk. Precautionary measures start with a layering system of clothing, including fleece jackets, wool shirts, synthetic underwear, or other fabrics that retain body heat when they are damp and wick moisture away from the skin. People can lose up to two-thirds of their body heat through their heads, so pack warm fleece or wool hats for your children, even on short dayhikes.

The first symptom of hypothermia is shivering. Other early warnings are slurred speech, mild confusion, and loss of coordination. As the body's core temperature falls, the victim stops shivering, becomes more confused, and is subject to irrational behavior, such as removing his clothing.

Be sensitive to these behavior changes and at the first symptoms, take steps to warm the victim. Remember that kids are particularly vulnerable, because their smaller bodies can lose heat rapidly. Get them out of the water or wind, remove wet clothing, get a hat on their heads, and warm them with dry clothing or your own body heat. If you are near camp, start up the car heater or crawl inside a sleeping bag and hold them chest to chest. Encourage them to drink warm fluids.

People whose core temperature has plummeted appear in a stupor and are susceptible to ventricular fibrillation, the chaotic beating of the heart that can lead to death. Victims of advanced hypothermia should be taken to a hospital.

SHOCK

Any serious injury, such as broken bones resulting from a fall, heart attack, a car or boating accident or even snakebite can lead to shock. Shock is a serious condition that in cases of traumatic injury can quickly result in death unless immediate measures are taken to revive and stabilize the victim.

Treating shock requires that the rescuer be familiar with the ABC's of first aid treatment: clear the **a**irway, check for **b**reathing, and restore **c**irculation. It requires a knowledge of the basics of cardiopulmonary resuscitation (CPR). Referring to a thumbnail sketch in the pages of this or any other book is not a substitute for taking a course and becoming certified in CPR by the American Heart Association or the Red Cross.

The three basic steps in reviving a person who is not breathing and has no discernible heartbeat are:

- **One**, place the victim flat on his back and open the airway by lifting the chin.
- **Two**, if the victim still is not breathing, inflate the lungs by pinching the nostrils, placing your lips around his mouth, and administering two full breaths.
- **Three**, compress the chest by placing the heel of one hand against the sternum, placing the other hand on top of the first hand, and then pressing down sharply. To apply pressure, keep your shoulders aligned over your hands and your elbows locked. Do not compress the chest more than about two inches. Press at a rate of 80 compressions per minute. After 15 seconds, administer two more breaths, then repeat. Continue CPR until breathing and pulse are restored or medical help arrives.

To perform CPR on children, you must increase the rate of compressions. Depending upon the age, the method of applying pressure also changes (from heel of hand to fingers or thumbs), as does the depth to which you compress the chest. If you're planning to spend much time outdoors, take a course. Someday, it could save a life.

Most victims of shock die from blood loss, either by external bleeding or from internal injuries which may not be readily apparent. Try to control bleeding by applying direct pressure to the wound with a shirt or other clean material. If pressure alone does not control further blood loss, wrap the wound snugly with a broad bandage of clean cloth.

Stabilize the victim and slightly elevate the legs to promote the supply of venous blood to the chest and arterial flow to the head. Keep the victim warm and evacuate to a hospital unless medical help is on the way.

BONE FRACTURES, DISLOCATIONS, AND SPRAINS

Fractures and dislocations are serious injuries that should be treated by a doctor. Spinal injuries from falls during hikes or while horseback riding can result in paralysis, so it is extremely critical not to move any victim who has neck or back pain. Drape the injured person in a blanket or with warm clothing and go for help.

Collarbone and upper arm injuries are best treated by creating a makeshift sling out of a shirt or other piece of cloth and immobilizing the limb. Injuries to the fingers, forearms, or legs should be splinted. A splint can be made from any rigid object, such as an aluminum tent-pole section, a pencil (for broken fingers), or even a branch. A rolled-up or folded foam pad can also be used. Keep the splint in place with an elastic bandage or strips of cloth torn from a T-shirt. Be careful not to wrap the injured limb too tightly and cut off circulation. Don't attempt to "reset" the bone fracture by pulling unless you know what you are doing. Evacuate the victim to the nearest hospital.

Ankle sprains are probably the most common hiking injury. If the sprain occurs miles from camp, it's usually advisable to walk out without removing the shoe or boot. Once the sprained ankle swells, it will be difficult to replace the boot, making the trip back to camp that much more difficult. You may have to be firm with kids who recoil from the initial pain; stress to them that the sprain will hurt a lot more if they insist on resting for a couple of hours before turning back. Back in camp, apply ice to the ankle and keep it elevated to help reduce swelling. The pain and swelling of sprains usually subsides in about 48 hours, time enough to luxuriate in the hammock and read a couple of good books while others do the work for a change.

MINOR CUTS, CONTUSIONS, AND BLISTERS

Suffering minor cuts and scrapes is a normal part of camping. To treat superficial cuts that do not damage underlying tendons or ligaments, follow three simple steps:

- First, stop bleeding by applying direct pressure to the wound.
- Second, wash with clean water and a disinfectant.
- Apply a bandage to keep dirt from infecting the wound. (**Note:** Always apply bandages to your children's cuts and scrapes, even the minor ones. The placebo effect is astonishing.)

Usually there is no need to close minor cuts with emergency stitching. In fact, closing minor cuts is generally discouraged, because it can trap dirt inside the wound. Cuts about the face and scalp are the exception, since they often need to be closed to stop bleeding and are less prone to infection. Long hair is an advantage for scalp-wound victims, because strands of hair can be tied together to keep the cut closed. Super Glue is another option for uncontaminated wounds where you don't want scarring. Apply continuous pressure for at least ten minutes to control bleeding, then hold wound edges together and seal with a thin layer of glue.

Severe bruising of tender tissues under the thumb and fingernails is a common camp injury incurred while hammering—and missing—tent stakes. The resulting pressure of ruptured blood vessels causes intense swelling, which can be alleviated by piercing the nail with a red-hot needle.

To prevent foot blisters along the trail, buy hiking boots that fit and break them in before your trip. Avoid wearing cotton socks, which absorb sweat and stick to the skin. Wear two layers of socks, with the inner liner made of Thermax, polypropylene, acrylic, or other moisture-wicking material. That way, the friction occurs between the layers of fabric. Foot powder or antiperspirant deodorant also help to keep feet dry and prevent blistering.

Usually, you can feel the rubbing of an abrasion before a blister appears. Stop as soon as any member of the family begins to complain and bandage the red spot before proceeding. Use white athletic tape if you have it; tape stays

A parent's caring touch and a well-stocked medical supply kit can go a long way to easing the pain of a child's cut or bruise.

on better than conventional bandages. Don't lance blisters. Just cleanse them thoroughly with soap and water and apply a thin layer of Spenco Second Skin. Cover with a piece of moleskin.

CHOKING

Thousands of Americans die each year choking on food, usually while trying to swallow unchewed pieces of meat. Try to keep the dinner atmosphere in camp quiet, because kids who are laughing and talking while they eat are particularly susceptible.

Don't attempt to aid people who are making a lot of noise while choking; they are still breathing and coming to their aid may only cause the obstruction to lodge in the airway. But if the choking subsides and a person can no longer breathe, begins to turn blue, or grasps at his neck with his hands, only prompt application of the Heimlich maneuver can prevent death.

To perform the Heimlich maneuver, grasp the person from behind and press one fist against his stomach above the navel. Place your other hand on top of the fist and pull in and up in a series of short, hard jerks. If the obstruction persists and the victim loses consciousness, open the mouth, reach in with a forefinger, and attempt to hook it behind the obstruction. If you are alone in camp, perform the Heimlich maneuver on yourself or grasp a fallen log or rock and lean sharply against it or jerk it against your stomach.

To clear the airway of an infant, lay him across your forearm with his head down and slap him or her with the heel of your hand between the shoulder blades.

DEHYDRATION

Most people associate dehydration with being lost in the desert and having nothing to drink. In fact, most campers who become dehydrated have plenty of water; they just don't drink enough of it to replace the fluids and electrolytes lost through sweating during heavy exercise. Diarrhea and vomiting also are common causes of dehydration.

Dehydration is much easier to prevent than treat. An adult needs lots of water, at least two liters during long dayhikes. If you can't carry that much, then bring iodine tablets or a filter pump to purify stream water found along the trail. Have kids drink during every rest stop rather than only when they become thirsty. If you wait until you are thirsty to drink, you are already on the road to dehydration. The body can absorb fluids better in small amounts, so take a few swallows every half hour or so rather than emptying a canteen all at once.

Sports drinks help replace electrolyte loss, so it's a good idea to add a tablespoon or so of a drink mix to your water bottles when filling up. You can improvise by adding a teaspoon or so of salt and sugar to your drinking water. However, be aware that sports drinks are not a substitute for plain water, which your body also needs to help eliminate wastes.

SUNBURN AND HEAT-RELATED ILLNESSES

People's susceptibility to sunburn varies widely, with redheads and blue-eyed blondes being most at risk. If you or your children are sensitive, schedule hikes and other activities for early mornings and evenings and try to stay out of direct sunlight during the hours of greatest intensity (usually between 9 A.M. and 3 P.M.). Wear hats, long-sleeved shirts, and pants, and liberally apply sunscreen with an SPF power of at least 15. Don't forget the tops of feet, backs of legs, and behind the ears. Some kids are sensitive to PABA, an ingredient in most suntan lotions. If their skin shows an allergic reaction, buy a lotion that is PABA-free.

Remember that skin burns more easily at high altitudes. Boaters must be extremely careful, because in addition to overhead sunlight, they are subject to sunlight bouncing from the water's surface onto their faces.

Many touted sunburn remedies, such as calamine lotion and anesthetic sprays, offer short-term relief at best. Some mentholated creams do offer longer relief and aspirin, ibuprofen, or acetaminophen (recommended for smaller children) will help. Aloe vera lotion works if applied frequently.

Cramps caused by heat and other related illnesses are usually a result of hiking or other physical exertion by people who have traveled to their campground from cooler climates and are not acclimated to the heat. Drinking fluids help, but an ounce of prevention isn't nearly enough. It takes lots of water to replace the fluids and electrolytes lost during sweating. Give yourself a urine test. If yours isn't copious and clear, you aren't taking in enough fluids. It also helps to wear light-colored clothing that doesn't absorb heat and rest in the shade frequently during long hikes. Rinse your clothing out in ponds, streams, or drinking water to get some evaporative cooling under way.

Many who are not acclimated will suffer from swollen hands, ankles, and feet. This is generally not serious and the swelling usually subsides within several days. Elderly people, who are particularly sensitive to swelling and heat exhaustion, should seriously consider camping in a small motorhome or trailer that runs air conditioning off a generator.

Learn to recognize the symptoms of heat exhaustion (nausea, headaches, rapid pulse, clammy skin, and light-headedness) and of heat stroke (high temperature combined with dry skin). Treat both by getting the victim into the shade and having him drink lots of water. If you suspect someone is suffering from heat stroke, strip his clothes off and cool the skin with rags or clothing soaked in water. Heat stroke can be fatal unless you bring down the soaring body temperature.

TROUBLE IN THE WELL

The microscopic protozoan cyst that causes *Giardia*, the backpacker's curse, is deposited into water sources by the feces of animals. Even the crystal threads of mountain tributaries can be contaminated. For this reason any water you intend to drink along the trail must be purified, either by boiling, filtration, or the addition of chemical halogens such as iodine and chlorine.

Most experts recommend boiling water for 10 minutes, especially at higher altitudes where water boils at a lower temperature. The addition of iodine tablets is probably the cheapest, easiest water to purify water. However, it can take up to an hour for an iodine tab to purify a quart of water (the colder the water, the longer it takes to kill the cyst). Filter pumps are very effective at removing *Giardia* cysts, but are relatively expensive and take up more room in your daypack. L.L. Bean offers compact micro-filters that work well for dayhikes and occasional use.

The days have passed when we can freely drink water directly from an outdoor water source. The microscopic Giardia *cyst has been found nearly everywhere, even in high mountain streams. A water purification filter is the quickest and easiest way to procure pure water while camping.*

Children are particularly vulnerable to *Giardia*, not only because they may be more tempted to drink from a creek, but because they accidentally swallow water while swimming.

Although medical treatment to cure *Giardia* is simple and effective, the malady can be difficult to diagnose because the cyst has a long incubation time (from a few days to several weeks) and does not always show up in the stool sample analysis. After one camping trip, my 11-year-old nephew began to suffer from nausea and lost weight steadily for half a year, despite undergoing a battery of medical tests. Because he did not have diarrhea, which is the obvious indicator, the real cause was unsuspected. Finally, my brother Kevin, who is an emergency room physician, had him tested for *Giardia* and the results turned up positive. If your child has similar symptoms or suffers from a general malaise after a camping expedition, suspect a waterborne illness sooner rather than later.

Swimmer's itch is caused by the *Schistosoma* parasite, which is common in many still waters, particularly in algae-infested lakes and ponds. Although uncomfortable, the symptoms, which can be relieved with antihistamines, generally clear up without medical treatment.

MOTION SICKNESS

My daughter sometimes becomes nauseous on the road during camping trips. If she rides in the front passenger seat during the windiest parts of the road and we stop occasionally, she is usually able to get through the trip without incident. Other tricks, such as fixing the eyes on the horizon, also work to varying degrees for people subject to motion sickness. Many fishermen swear by acupressure bands worn on the wrists to subdue nausea on rough seas. Carbonated cola drinks and ginger ale may also help calm the stomach.

If these remedies don't work, there are a number of effective over-the-counter medications available in pill form or as ear patches which release small amounts of nausea-inhibiting drugs over several days. Many, like Dramamine, can make the user drowsy. Some don't cause drowsiness, but may have other side effects. Ask a pharmacist to recommend the medication that may be appropriate for you or your child.

DIARRHEA AND CONSTIPATION

Diarrhea and constipation are two of the most common maladies that befall campers, the first from a change in water source and the second from a change in diet.

Treat diarrhea with Pepto-Bismol or Imodium. Drink lots of fluids, especially sports drinks such as Gatorade that contain electrolytes. Constipation can be more difficult to diagnose, especially in children. The most common symptom is belly pain on the left side (the opposite side from the appendix). To avoid constipation, eat lots of fruits, vegetables, and whole grains during the trip. Mild constipation can be relieved with milk of Magnesia. Dulcolax suppositories can be purchased without a prescription and are the answer for severe cramps.

EYE CARE

The dust and grit that swirl about many campgrounds, as well as campfire sparks, are among the leading causes of eye injuries. Flush foreign particles out of the eye with water. If pain persists, the eye should be patched overnight. Sufferers of eye abrasions will be sensitive to direct sunlight for several days, but if pain persists past 24 hours or so, a particle of grit may have become embedded in the cornea. It should be removed by a physician.

Wearing glasses is the first line of defense against eye injuries and damage from ultraviolet radiation. The L.L. Bean catalog lists several models of sunglasses with 100-percent UV protection; don't settle for less than 85 percent. Avoid cheap plastic kids' sunglasses that don't list UV protection on the label.

Eye protection is crucial for hiking at high altitude, where the sun's rays are very intense. Fishermen and boaters should wear sunglasses with a polarizing filter to reduce glare from the water's surface. Glare from snow can be just as damaging as glare from water, so eye protection is important during winter camping trips or hikes where snow fields are encountered.

MEDICAL KITS

Parents should pack a small medical kit during dayhikes, as well as a more fully stocked kit in the car. L.L. Bean offers several medical kits that fit both bills. Campers who want to put together their own kits should consult the reference section at the end of this book for a list of recommended contents.

AFTERWORD

Ashes to Riches

"Ah, this is bullier yet!"
THEODORE ROOSEVELT, UPON AWAKENING DURING A CAMPING TRIP
WITH JOHN MUIR TO FIND HIMSELF BURIED UNDER SNOW

In the movie "Parenthood," Mary Steenburgen plays a woman who is run ragged by the misadventures of her children, but glows with happiness in her role as a mother, anyway.

"Life is messy," she declares to her fastidious husband, Steve Martin.

"I hate messy," he says, "it's so"—his face contorts in a grimace—"messy."

Camping is messy, too. That is one reason it comes so naturally to people who have children, who long ago gave up wiping water marks off the table top—or contemplating the meaning of life, for that matter—having lost the time for such trivial pursuits in the face of getting through the day.

Many instructional books paint an unrelentingly sunny vision of camping. Their writers tend to equate happiness with order, when in my experience, it is more often built upon the ashes of a day when everything seemed to go wrong. I hope I have not made the same mistake, because if there is one point I'd like to leave you with, it is that the rewards of pitching a tent with your children have nothing to do with a trip going exactly as planned. The truth is that camping brings a family together not just because it is fun, but also because all the members must work together in order to fully enjoy living outdoors. Memories are made of mistakes, and the steak that is fished out of the fire will taste better in the telling a few months down the road than one that is cooked without incident.

The important thing to remember is that even the most trying day is succeeded by the dawn. When you step out of the tent and boil the first cup of camp coffee you've had in al-

149

Camping's most memorable moments are like falling stars. You can't see them coming, and the only way to enjoy them is to keep your eyes and mind open.

most a year, all the tribulations of the packing and the traveling—the bathing suit your daughter forgot and you drove ten miles back home to retrieve, the bad fast food you ate because the cooler was packed under so much gear you would have needed a backhoe to unearth it, the lopsided ground you slept on because all the good spots were taken when you finally pulled into the campground—are suddenly far away. Even the house you left seems to exist in past tense, exiled to the farthest recesses of memory, along with the worries of work and the ceaseless bustle of urban existence.

Standing with the coffee cup in your hand, you feel relaxed for the first time in months. It is as if an invisible weight has been lifted off your chest and a film over your eyes has peeled to reveal a clarity of vision that is almost childlike in its wonder. You look around the camp and notice that a few other families are packing up; after breakfast, you can move the tent to one of several flat sites near the riverbank. The current is high from rain and you find yourself drawn to it, compelled to listen to the notes of its song. Then a kingfisher darts to the surface and lifts, shedding diamonds of water from its wings, a silver minnow flashing in its bill.

You turn to see the first sleepy head poke out of the tent.

It all seems so *right*. You take a deep breath of cool, clean air. You look beyond the tent to the ridge of the pines, into the azure sky above, and wonder why you let so much time go by before bringing the family back up here.

It is at moments like this that a question occurs, one that may have seemed inconceivable only a few hours before. Is it possible that life gets any better than this?

Then you glance over at the canoe, dinged on the bottom where you flipped it last year, and decide not to tempt fate by answering this particular question out loud.

SECTION
IV

References

Appendix

CAMP GEAR CHECKLIST

- Tent, poles, stakes, and ground cloth
- Rain fly
- Sleeping bags (1 per person)
- Sleeping pads
- Pillows
- Cookstove
- Cookbox with pots, pans, utensils, and scrub pad
- Cooler and food boxes
- Lantern and spare mantles.
- Extra fuel bottle or propane canister, depending upon type of lantern
- Rain parkas (1 per person)
- Backpacks or belt packs for dayhikes
- Ax
- Swede or bow saw for cutting logs
- Flashlights (1 per person)
- Camp chairs
- Binoculars
- Fishing gear
- Folding knife
- Sportsman's multipurpose tool or Swiss Army knife

- Polarized sunglasses
- Medicine kit
- Sunscreen
- Insect repellent
- Plastic trashcan liners (a hundred and one uses, i.e., emergency parka, emergency waders, water bag, fish bag)
- Duct tape (likewise)
- Water containers
- Fire grill
- Charcoal and lighter fluid (for cooking and lighting fires from damp wood)
- Lightweight, folding Army shovel
- 100 feet of parachute cord or strong nylon rope
- Bungee cords
- Work gloves
- Folding camp table
- Air-freshener packets (for outhouse) and favorite-brand toilet paper
- Broom
- Mesh bug tent
- Portable shower
- Guitar or harmonica
- Hammock
- Camera
- Comforters

CHILDREN'S CHECKLIST

- Portable toilets for young children
- Diaper bag for infants
- Favorite toys and stuffed animals
- Playing cards and board games
- Whiffle bat and ball
- Frisbee
- Books
- Sing-along books
- Children's flotation mattresses
- Mask, snorkel, and flippers
- Life jackets

- Kite
- Extra shoes or wading sandals

COOKBOX CONTENTS

- 12-inch cold-handled steel skillet (cold-handled skillets have a long handle with an alloy sheath that doesn't get hot, making them more suitable for cooking over a fire than regular skillets)
- 10-inch nonstick skillet (ideal for pancakes)
- 3-quart steel or aluminum pot with lid
- 1-quart steel or aluminum pot with lid
- Plastic cups for each camper (each person gets a different color)
- Coffee mugs for adults and children's hot chocolate (insulated plastic mugs with lids are good in case the cup gets knocked over; they also keep drinks hot longer on chilly mornings)
- Coffee pot (blue-enamel or steel)
- Knife, fork, and spoon for every camper
- Flat Tupperware container for cooking utensils
- Steel spatula (for steel skillet)
- Plastic spatula (for nonstick skillet)
- Metal plate to use in food preparation, as cutting board with heavy paper plate inside and as makeshift holder for hot coals
- Kitchen knife (the folding Opinel knife with wooden handle and lock-back design is the camp knife nonpareil. Get the model with the 5-inch blade for cookbox; the smaller #8 model for your pocket. Neither should set you back more than $12.)
- Corkscrew and can opener (if you have a Swiss Army knife *and* strong hands, separate tools are unnecessary)
- 1 roll heavy-duty foil
- Heavy-duty paper plates
- Plastic or aluminum cereal bowls
- 2 rolls paper towels (spare roll can be stored in food box)
- Biodegradable dishwashing soap (optional)
- Kitchen scrub sponge
- 6 plastic grocery bags for sheathing pots and skillets that are blackened by fire
- 6 tall kitchen garbage bags
- 2 pot holders
- Small dish towel
- Tablecloth

- Apron (a good idea if working over a fire; helps keep food odors off clothing in bear country and makes the camp cook look professional)
- Small wooden cutting board (optional)
- Box of wooden matches
- 2 pie-irons (pack flat on the floorboards of van or car)
- 10-inch cast-iron Dutch oven, (optional, stored underneath car seat until needed)

DAYPACK CONTENTS

- Sunscreen
- Insect repellent
- Whistles (for emergency signaling)
- Matches
- Fire starter
- Compass and map for extended hikes
- Mini flashlight (extra bulb and batteries)
- Lightweight space blanket
- Extra jacket (fleece or other material that maintains body warmth when wet)
- Knife
- Strong nylon cord
- Candle
- Hat for sun and warmth
- Water filter or iodine tablets for water purification
- Water container
- Trail food
- Sunglasses with UV protection
- Rain parkas
- Medical kit

HIKERS' MEDICAL KIT*

- Bandages for minor cuts and scrapes
- Four-inch square sterile gauze pads (2, extra thick)
- Tiny scissors or scalpel blade (for shaving calluses, draining abscesses, lancing blisters, cutting away dead skin)
- Tweezers for splinters

- Sharp surgical needle (for removing splinters, prickly pear spines, etc.)
- Antibacterial or iodine wipe
- Antibacterial ointment (Polysporin recommended)
- Moleskin and Spenco Second Skin for blisters
- Super Glue for closing lacerations
- White athletic tape to stabilize sprained ankles and apply bandages
- Aspirin and acetaminophen (for fever, pain, headaches, altitude sickness, etc.)
- Motrin or ibuprofen (for fever, pain, and use as anti-inflammatory)
- Adhesive tape
- First aid booklet

CAR MEDICAL KIT*
(in addition to contents listed above)

- Pocket mask for CPR
- Lightweight splint with elastic bandages for wrapping sprains
- Thermometer
- Duct tape (makeshift splints, especially for immobilizing head in cases of spine injury by taping head to board)
- Latex gloves
- Silvadene or aloe vera-based burn ointment
- Antihistamine (Benadryl) for hives, insect stings, and as a sleep aid
- Pepto Bismol or Imodium for diarrhea
- Antacid (Maalox, Mylanta, Tums)
- Tinactin for athlete's foot, jock itch, to kill fungus
- Hydrocortisone cream for poison ivy, insect stings
- Personal medications

---

*L.L. Bean offers several medical kits for hikers and campers.

References

PRODUCTS

My prejudices for certain types of camp gear are reflected throughout this book, but keep in mind that any one person's experience is limited to a very small fraction of the market. There are many tents, sleeping bags, cookstoves, portable showers, and other products I've never had the opportunity to use, and many more that will be developed over the next several years.

L.L. Bean takes pride in field testing its products to ensure that they are both reliable and user-friendly. Their catalogs list a complete selection of camping gear and cooking supplies, ranging from practical, inexpensive gear to the most innovative designs. The L.L. Bean store, located in Freeport, Maine, is open 24 hours a day, 365 days a year. Whether you visit in person or order by phone, the staff will be happy to help you choose equipment to fit your family's needs and budget. All merchandise is unconditionally guaranteed.

To place an order or request a catalog, call 1-800-221-4221. Representatives are available 24 hours a day, every day of the year. You can shop on-line at *www.llbean.com*.

OUTDOOR SCHOOLS

L.L. Bean's Outdoor Discovery Schools offer instruction in backpacking, canoeing, kayaking, flyfishing, wilderness first aid, outdoor photography, wing shooting, mountain biking, bushwhacking, and navigation with map and compass, with special programs for children and for parents with children. For information, call 1-800-341-4341, ext. 26666 or write to the L.L. Bean Outdoor Discovery Schools, Freeport, ME 04033.

Other outdoor education schools with excellent reputations are:

- Outward Bound
  R.R. 2, Box 280
  Garrison, NY 10524-9757
  1-914-424-4000

- NOLS, the National Outdoor Leadership Schools
  288 Main St.
  Lander, WY 82520
  1-307-332-8800

Contact NOLS for information on the *Leave No Trace* principles of camping and backcountry use. Or phone *Leave No Trace* at 1-800-332-4100 to obtain booklets for wise outdoor use specific to the region you intend to visit.

CONSERVATION ORGANIZATIONS

These conservation organizations sponsor many outdoor education programs and offer superlative publications and activities for club members.

- National Wildlife Federation (NWF)
  1400 16th St. NW
  Washington, DC 20036
  1-202-797-6800

  (Members may receive a subscription to *Ranger Rick,* an excellent wildlife magazine for children).

- Nature Conservancy
  1815 N. Lynn St.
  Arlington, VA 22209
  1-703-841-5300

- Sierra Club
  85 Second St. (2nd floor)
  San Francisco, CA 94105
  1-415-977-5500

- Wilderness Society
  900 17th St. NW
  Washington, DC 20006
  1-202-833-2300

HIKING AND CAMPING ORGANIZATIONS

Two organizations that provide excellent resource material for hikers and campers and publish helpful periodicals for members include:

- American Hiking Society
  1422 Fenwick Lane
  Silver Springs, MD 20910
  1-301-565-6704

- Appalachian Mountain Club
  5 Joy St.
  Boston, MA 02108
  1-617-523-0636

MAGAZINES

- *Camping Life* (published 6 times a year)
  P.O. Box 392
  Mt. Morris, ILL 61054
  1-800-786-2721

- *Rodale's Guide to Family Camping* (published biannually)
  Rodale Press
  33 Minor St.
  Emmaus, PA 18098
  1-610-967-5171

- *Family Camping*
  33 Minor St.
  Emmaus, PA 18098
  1-610-967-5171

WHERE-TO-GO CAMPING BOOKS

A number of books giving detailed descriptions of thousands of campgrounds and hikes are published by Foghorn Press. Among the titles are included: *Southwest Camping, The Complete Guide to Pacific Northwest Camping, The Best in Tent Camping: Washington and Oregon, California Camping, Baja Camping, Pacific Northwest Hiking, Rocky Mountain Camping, Utah and Nevada Camping, Easy Camping in Northern California, Easy Hiking in Northern California,* and *The Camper's Companion.* Contact Foghorn Press at 555 DeHaro St., The Boiler Room (Suite 220), San Francisco, CA 94107.

Woodall's Campground Directory updates information on thousands of campgrounds annually. The address is 13975 West Polo Trail Drive, Lake Forest, IL 60045.

Cottage Publications (420 South 4th St., Elkhart, IN 46516-2748, phone 1-800-272-5518) publishes several books by Don Wright, including *Don Wright's Guide to Free Campgrounds* and *Camping on a Shoestring*, available in both western and eastern editions.

FAMILY CAMPING BOOKS

- *Camping for Kids* by Stephen and Elizabeth Griffin. NorthWord Press, 1994.

- *Parents' Guide to Hiking and Camping, A Trailside Guide* by Alice Cary. W.W. Norton and Co., 500 5th Avenue, New York, NY 10110.

- *Simple Tent Camping* by Zora and David Aiken. Ragged Mountain Press, Camden, ME. 1996.

- *Camping With Kids* by Don Wright. Cottage Publications, Inc., 420 S. 4th St., Elkhart, IN 46516-2748. 1992.

- *Roughing It Easy* by Dian Thomas. The Dian Thomas Publishing Co., Holladay, Utah.

- *The Camper's and Backpacker's Bible* by Tom Huggler. Doubleday, 1540 Broadway, New York, NY 10036. 1995.

- *Camping and Backpacking with Children* by Steven Boga. Stackpole Books. 1995.

INTERNET REFERENCE

To date, one of best outdoor reference pages on the Internet is GORP (Great Outdoor Recreation Page) at *www.gorp.com*. Another is CampUSA at *www.CampUSA.com.*, which is a locater service for finding campgrounds nationwide. Because Internet web sites turn over at a rapid rate, the best idea is to make a key-word search for current listings.

FEDERAL LAND AGENCIES

You can make activity-specific searches, including camping, for all federal lands through a single web site on the Internet at *www.recreation.com*.

- National Forest Service (NFS)
  U.S. Department of Agriculture
  P.O. Box 96090
  Washington, DC 20090-6090
  1-202-205-0957

- National Park Service (NPS)
  P.O. Box 37127
  Washington, DC 20013-7127
  1-202-347-5668

- National Wildlife Refuge (NWR)
  U.S. Fish and Wildlife Service
  Washington, DC
  1-202-208-4354

- Bureau of Land Management (BLM)
  Department of the Interior
  1849 C Street N.W.
  Washington, DC 20240-0001
  1-202-452-0330

- Bureau of Reclamation
  Box 043
  550 West Fort St.
  Boise, ID 83724

- U.S. Army Corps of Engineers
  3909 Halls Ferry Rd.
  Vicksburg, MS 39180-6199

STATE PARK SYSTEMS

Campground reservations can be made for many state parks. Because the addresses and phone numbers for state agencies are in a constant state of flux, many of the numbers below will soon be outdated. Try the Tourism Division numbers first. Call information for new listings.

- Alabama Department of Conservation and Natural Resources
  Montgomery, AL
  1-800-252-7275

- Alaska Division of Parks and Outdoor Recreation
  Anchorage, AK
  1-907-269-8701

- Arizona State Parks
  Phoenix, AZ
  1-602-542-4174

- Arkansas State Parks
  Little Rock, AR
  1-501-682-7777

- Colorado Department of Natural Resources
  State Parks Division
  1-303-866-3437

- Connecticut Department of Economic Development
  Rocky Hill, CT
  1-800-CT-BOUND

- Delaware Department of Natural Resources
  Division of Parks and Recreation
  Dover, DE
  1-302-739-4702

- Florida Division of Tourism
  Tallahassee, FL
  1-850-488-5607

- Georgia Department of Natural Resources
  Division of State Parks
  1-404-656-3530

- Hawaii Department of Land and Natural Resources
  State Parks Division
  1-808-587-0400

- Idaho Division of Tourism Development
  Boise, ID
  1-800-635-7820

- Illinois Department of Natural Resources
  Springfield, IL
  1-217-782-1395

- Indiana Department of Natural Resources
  Indianapolis, IN
  1-317-232-4124
  Hoosier Camper (camping information)
  1-800-837-7842

- Iowa Department of Natural Resources
  Des Moines, IA
  1-515-281-5918
  Division of Tourism
  1-800-345-IOWA

- Kansas Department of Wildlife and Parks
  Topeka, KS
  1-316-672-5911
  Division of Tourism
  1-800-252-6727

- Kentucky Department of Fish and Wildlife Resources
Frankfort, KY
1-800-858-1549
Department of Travel Development
1-800-225-TRIP

- Louisiana State Parks Office
Baton Rouge, LA
1-888-677-1400

- Maine Bureau of Parks and Land
Augusta, ME
1-207-287-3821

- Maryland Department of Natural Resources
Annapolis, MD
1-410-260-8186
Office of Tourism Development
1-800-543-1036

- Massachusetts Office of Travel and Tourism
Boston, MA
1-800-227-MASS

- Michigan Department of Natural Resources
Lansing, MI
1-517-373-9900
Travel Bureau
1-800-5432-YES

- Minnesota Department of Natural Resources
St. Paul, MN
1-651-296-6157
Office of Tourism
1-800-657-3700

- Mississippi Department of Wildlife, Fisheries and Parks
Jackson, MS
1-601-364-2120

- Missouri Department of Natural Resources
Jefferson City, MO
1-800-334-6946
Division of Tourism
1-800-877-1234

- Montana Department of Fish, Wildlife and Parks
Helena, MT
1-406-444-2535
Travel Montana
1-800-541-1447

- Nebraska Game and Parks Commission
  Lincoln, NE
  1-402-471-0641

- Nevada Tourism
  Carson City, NV
  1-800-NEVADA-8

- New Hampshire Office of Travel and Tourism
  Concord, NH
  1-800-386-4664

- New Jersey Division Parks and Forestry
  Trenton, NJ
  1-609-292-2797
  Division of Travel and Tourism
  1-800-JERSEY-7

- New Mexico Department of Fish and Game
  Santa Fe, NM
  1-800-862-9310
  Department of Tourism
  1-800-545-2040

- New York State Parks
  Albany, NY
  1-800-456-CAMP

- North Carolina Wildlife Resources Commission
  Raleigh, NC
  1-919-733-3391
  Division of Travel and Tourism
  1-800-VISIT-NC

- North Dakota Game and Fish Department
  Bismarck, ND
  1-701-328-6300
  Tourism Promotion
  1-800-HELLO-ND

- Ohio Department of Natural Resources
  Columbus, OH
  1-614-265-7000
  Division of Travel and Tourism
  1-800-BUCKEYE

- Oklahoma Department of Wildlife Conservation
  Oklahoma City, OK
  1-405-521-3851
  Tourism and Recreation Department
  1-800-652-6552

- Oregon Info Hotline (general camping information)
  1-800-551-6949
  Oregon and Washington State Parks (campground reservations)
  1-800-452-5687

- Pennsylvania Bureau of Travel Marketing
  1-800-VISIT-PA
  Pennsylvania Tourism Office
  1-800-564-5009

- Rhode Island Tourism Office
  Providence, RI
  1-800-556-2484

- South Carolina State Parks and Recreation, Tourism Office
  Columbia, SC
  1-803-734-4135

- South Dakota Department of Tourism
  Pierre, SD
  1-800-SDAKOTA
  State Parks
  1-800-710-CAMP

- Tennessee State Parks
  Nashville, TN
  1-888-TN-PARKS

- Texas State Parks Information
  Austin, TX
  1-800-792-1112

- Utah Division of State Parks and Recreation
  Salt Lake City, UT
  1-801-538-7220

- Vermont Travel Division
  Montpelier, VT
  1-800-VERMONT

- Virginia Tourism
  Richmond, VA
  1-800-VISIT-VA
  Virginia Campground Guide
  1-800-922-6782

- Washington Info Hot Line (general camping information)
  1-800-233-0321
  Washington State Parks (reservations)
  1-800-452-5687

- West Virginia
  Division of Tourism and Parks
  Charleston, WV
  1-304-259-5216

- Wisconsin Department of Natural Resources
  Bureau of Parks and Recreation
  Madison, WI
  1-608-266-2181
  Division of Tourism
  1-800-432-TRIP

- Wyoming Game and Fish Department
  Cheyenne, WY
  1-307-777-4600
  Division of Tourism
  1-800-225-5996

CANADIAN PROVINCES

Alberta

- Travel Alberta
  Edmonton, Alberta
  1-800-661-8888

British Columbia

- Ministry of Tourism and Recreation
  Victoria, British Columbia
  1-800-663-6000
  Discovery Camping (Provincial Parks reservations)
  1-800-689-9025

Manitoba

- Manitoba Natural Resources
  Winnipeg, Manitoba
  1-800-214-6497
  Travel Manitoba
  1-800-665-0040

New Brunswick

- New Brunswick Tourism, Recreation and Heritage
  Fredericton, New Brunswick
  1-800-561-0123

Newfoundland and Labrador

- Department of Development and Tourism
  St. John's, Newfoundland
  1-800-563-6353

Northwest Territories

- Travel Arctic
  Yellowknife, Northwest Territories
  1-800-661-0788

Nunavut

- Nunavut Tourism
  1-800-491-7910

Ontario

- Ministry of Tourism and Recreation
  Toronto, Ontario
  1-800-668-2746

Prince Edward Island

- Department of Tourism and Parks
  Charlottetown, PEI
  1-800-463-4734

Quebec

- Tourism Quebec
  Quebec City, Quebec
  1-800-363-7777

Saskatchewan

- Tourism Saskatchewan
  Regina, Saskatchewan
  1-800-667-7191

Yukon Territories

- Tourism Yukon
  Whitehorse, Yukon Territories
  1-800-789-8566

Photo Credits

Photographs on pages xi, 6, 13, 14, 20, 21, 24 (top), 25, 26, 31, 33, 38, 49, 50, 61, 62 (right), 66, 68, 71, 74, 77, 83, 86, 88, 92, 93, 95–97, 102 (top), 107, 109, 111, 112, 117 (top), 120, 123, 129 courtesy of Jim Rowinski

Photographs on pages 4, 8, 9, 28, 47, 52, 56, 62 (left), 82, 114, 125, 132, 142, 150 courtesy of Adventure Photo & Film

Photographs on pages 16, 18, 102 (bottom), 105 (both), 113, 117 (bottom), 128, 137, 139 courtesy of Keith McCafferty

Photographs on pages 30, 51, 60 courtesy of L.L. Bean

Photographs on pages x (bottom), xii courtesy of Ken Redding

Photographs on page x (top) courtesy of Ben Kerns

Photograph on page 24 (bottom) courtesy of Tony Stone Images

Photograph on page 145 courtesy of Mike Brinson

Acknowledgments

I thank my wife, Gail Schontzler, for her love and support during this project and for her invaluable help editing the manuscript. I'm also indebted to my brother, Kevin McCafferty, who lent his expertise as an emergency room physician to the chapter concerning health and safety. And many thanks to my good friends Steve and Dale Dunn, who handed me the keys.

My memories and writing have been greatly enriched by all who have shared a campground or a tent with me. Many names have been forgotten, but there are some whose presence will never fade from my life. So thank you to Mike Czaja, "Florida" John Davis, Bernie Kurley, Bob and Duncan Bullock (and Bo, Lisa and Erin), the great Joe Gutkoski, "Snitty" and Twila Sizemore, Bill Morris, Keith Shein, John Izard, Mel and Kim Kotur (and Dan and Mike), Ray McVicker, Jerry Derring, Morice Booth, Louie Stoner, Vicki Ankney, "Bic," Gordon and Kay Wallace, Dave Myer, Bruce Milnes, John Hirvela, "Slick," Linda McCafferty, Brent and Brandon McCafferty, the California Schontzler gang, Robert Mussey, Carol Stocker, Becky Titcomb, Gigi Wilson, Drick Boyd, Dave Paylor, Marina Braswell, Karen and Bill Basil, Carly and Trevor Basil, Luke Bovenizer and Mason Bradley and his daughters, who flitted about the campground like moths in their diaphanous nightgowns and stole the hearts of all who had eyes for children.

I'd also like to thank my editor, Bryan Oettel, at Lyons Press, who made many helpful suggestions and patiently coaxed this book into shape.

Index